NEW STUDIES IN BIBLICAL THEOLOGY

MW00584480

Preaching in the
New Testament

NEW STUDIES IN BIBLICAL THEOLOGY 42

Series editor: D. A. Carson

Preaching in the New Testament

AN EXEGETICAL AND BIBLICAL-THEOLOGICAL STUDY

Jonathan I. Griffiths

APOLLOS

INTERVARSITY PRESS
DOWNERS GROVE, ILLINOIS 60515

APOLLOS (an imprint of Inter-Varsity Press, England)
36 Causton Street
London SW1P 4ST, England
Website: www.ivpbooks.com
Email: ivp@ivpbooks.com

InterVarsity Press, USA
P.O. Box 1400
Downers Grove, IL 60515, USA
Website: www.ivpress.com
Email: email@ivpress.com

First published 2017

Set in Monotype Times New Roman
Typeset in Great Britain by CRB Associates, Potterhanworth, Lincolnshire
Printed in the United States of America ∞

USA ISBN 978-0-8308-2643-8 (print)
USA ISBN 978-0-8308-8972-3 (digital)

UK ISBN 978-1-78359-491-7 (print)
UK ISBN 978-1-78359-492-4 (digital)

InterVarsity Press is committed to ecological stewardship and to the conservation of natural resources in all our operations. This book was printed using sustainably sourced paper.

British Library Cataloguing-in-Publication Data
A catalogue record for this book is available from the British Library.

Library of Congress Cataloging-in-Publication Data
Names: Griffiths, Jonathan (Preaching instructor), author.
Title: Preaching in the New Testament : an exegetical and
 biblical-theological study / Jonathan Griffiths.
Description: Downers Grove : InterVarsity Press, 2017. | Series: New studies
 in biblical theology ; 42 | Includes bibliographical references and index.
Identifiers: LCCN 2016046950 (print) | LCCN 2016051875 (ebook) | ISBN
 9780830826438 (pbk. : alk. paper) | ISBN 9780830889723 (eBook)
Subjects: LCSH: Preaching--Biblical teaching. | Bible. New
 Testament—Criticism, interpretation, etc.
Classification: LCC BS2545.P68 G75 2017 (print) | LCC BS2545.P68 (ebook) |
 DDC 251.009/015—dc23
LC record available at https://lccn.loc.gov/2016046950

P   25 24 23 22 21 20 19 18 17 16 15 14 13 12 11 10 9 8 7 6 5 4 3

Y   39 38 37 36 35 34 33 32 31 30 29 28 27 26 25 24 23 22 21 20 19

For my grandfather Gerald B. Griffiths
on the occasion of his ninety-fifth birthday

Contents

Series preface

New Studies in Biblical Theology is a series of monographs that address key issues in the discipline of biblical theology. Contributions to the series focus on one or more of three areas: (1) the nature and status of biblical theology, including its relations with other disciplines (e.g. historical theology, exegesis, systematic theology, historical criticism, narrative theology); (2) the articulation and exposition of the structure of thought of a particular biblical writer or corpus; and (3) the delineation of a biblical theme across all or part of the biblical corpora.

Above all, these monographs are creative attempts to help thinking Christians understand their Bibles better. The series aims simultaneously to instruct and to edify, to interact with the current literature and to point the way ahead. In God's universe, mind and heart should not be divorced: in this series we will try not to separate what God has joined together. While the notes interact with the best of scholarly literature, the text is uncluttered with untransliterated Greek and Hebrew, and tries to avoid too much technical jargon. The volumes are written within the framework of confessional evangelicalism, but there is always an attempt at thoughtful engagement with the sweep of the relevant literature.

Of the many books published every year on preaching, the overwhelming majority focus on the 'how to' fundamentals, mixed in with advice on preaching sermons from particular literary genres, the challenges of addressing a culture that is increasingly biblically illiterate, sage counsel on speaking on special occasions (e.g. Christmas, funerals, civic events), thoughtful insight on preaching Christologically or on preaching through specific biblical books, and the like. Relatively few, however, have attempted to think theologically about preaching itself (though see the book by Peter Adam, *Speaking God's Words*). This volume by Jonathan Griffiths addresses the need for a biblical theology of preaching by focusing on some foundational matters (the 'word of God' in the Bible, the language of 'preaching' in the New Testament, and the word ministries of all believers) before closely studying a handful of passages in Paul and in Hebrews. Considering how much preaching is done week by week around the world, it is good to have a study that requires us to reflect on what we are doing.

D. A. Carson
Trinity Evangelical Divinity School

Author's preface

This present work has been shaped significantly by my interactions with colleagues and students at the Proclamation Trust as we have thought together about the Bible's teaching about preaching and its proper place in the life of the church. It is a pleasure to record very special thanks to Tim Ward, Christopher Ash, Adrian Reynolds and David Jackman for their sage counsel, warm encouragement and significant editorial input. I have been helped also by friends and scholars from further afield who have kindly read the manuscript at various stages and have given valuable advice and suggestions for improvement, namely, Peter O'Brien, David Peterson and Peter Adam. Naturally, I bear responsibility for the limitations and shortcomings of this study, but it is unquestionably stronger because of the kind help I have received.

Jonathan Griffiths

Abbreviations

BDAG	W. Bauer, F. W. Danker, W. F. Arndt and F. W. Gingrich, *Geek–English Lexicon of the New Testament and Other Early Christian Literature*, 3rd ed., Chicago: University of Chicago Press, 1999
BDF	F. Blass, A. Debrunner and R. W. Funk, *A Greek Grammar of the New Testament and Other Early Christian Literature*, Chicago: University of Chicago Press, 1961
BNTC	Black's New Testament Commentaries
BST	The Bible Speaks Today
BT	*The Bible Translator*
EBC	Expositor's Bible Commentary
ESV	English Standard Version
Gk	Greek
HUCA	*Hebrew Union College Annual*
ICC	International Critical Commentary
IVPNTC	IVP New Testament Commentary Series
JBL	*Journal of Biblical Literature*
JETS	*Journal of the Evangelical Theological Society*
JSNT	*Journal for the Study of the New Testament*
JSNTSS	Journal for the Study of the New Testament Supplement Series
LNTS	Library of New Testament Studies
LS	H. G. Liddell and R. Scott, *A Greek–English Lexicon*, 8th ed., Oxford: Oxford University Press, 1897
LXX	Septuagint
Miss.	*Missiology: An International Review*
MM	J. H. Moulton and G. Milligan, *The Vocabulary of the Greek Testament*, London, 1914–1929
NA28	*Novum Testamentum Graece*, Nestle-Aland, 28th ed.
NETS	New English Translation of the Septuagint

NICNT	New International Commentary on the New Testament
NIGTC	New International Greek Testament Commentary
NIV	New International Version
NIVAC	NIV Application Commentary
NovT	*Novum Testamentum*
NovTSup	Novum Testamentum Supplement series
NSBT	New Studies in Biblical Theology
NT	New Testament
NTL	New Testament Library
NTS	*New Testament Studies*
OT	Old Testament
PBM	Paternoster Biblical Monographs
PBTM	Paternoster Biblical and Theological Monographs
PNTC	Pillar New Testament Commentary
SNTSMS	Society for New Testament Studies Monograph Series
SubBi	Subsidia biblica
TDNT	*Theological Dictionary of the New Testament*, ed. G. Kittel and G. Friedrich, tr. G. W. Bromiley, 10 vols, Grand Rapids: Eerdmans, 1964–1976
TDOT	*Theological Dictionary of the Old Testament*, ed. G. J. Botterweck, H. Ringgren and H.-J. Fabry, tr. J. T. Willis, G. W. Bromiley, D. E. Green and D. W. Stott, 15 vols, Grand Rapids: Eerdmans, 1974–2006
Them	*Themelios*
TynBul	*Tyndale Bulletin*
WBC	Word Biblical Commentary
WUNT	Wissenschaftliche Untersuchungen zum Neuen Testament
ZECNT	Zondervan Exegetical Commentary on the New Testament
ZNW	*Zeitschrift für die neutestamentliche Wissenschaft und die Kunde der älteren Kirche*

Introduction

Many reading this book would share the conviction that the preaching of the word of God is at the heart of God's plans for the gospel in our age; that it is vital for the health of the church; and that it is the central task of the pastor-teacher. However, many who share those convictions about preaching might struggle to articulate a fully adequate definition of preaching from Scripture. That has certainly been my own experience. And so it is right to ask: Could it be that such convictions concerning the distinctiveness and centrality of 'preaching' are simply grounded in a blend of history ('Think of the great preachers of the past . . .') and a heavy dose of pragmatism ('Preaching certainly seems to work . . .'), rather than in Scripture itself? History has much to teach us, and pragmatic concerns are not irrelevant, but neither history nor pragmatism must be allowed to control theology. The vital question is what Scripture says about this issue.

Why another book on preaching?

There are very many helpful books on preaching available in the evangelical marketplace.[1] The vast majority of these concern themselves primarily with the how-to of preaching. That is certainly an important issue to address, but that is not the interest or concern of this study. A much smaller number of books address primarily the character and theology of preaching according to Scripture.[2] In varying degrees of detail, such studies have traced the activity of the public declaration of God's word throughout Scripture and articulated the theological character of preaching in light of that broad sweep. Generally, they take it as basic that God has used the preaching of his word throughout the history of his dealings with his people, and so lessons we can learn from the phenomenon of preaching throughout Scripture

---

[1] A recent overview of some of the literature is offered in Meyer 2013: 316–333.
[2] Noteworthy contributions in recent years include Adam 1996; Meyer 2013; Ash 2009; Old 1998; see also Litfin's (2015) substantial but more narrowly focused exegetical study.

should shape and inform the practice of preaching in the contemporary, post-apostolic context. Such overviews are valuable, and it is not the purpose of this present study to recapitulate their findings.

However, two key, interrelated questions remain outstanding (from which a number of secondary questions will flow).

First, according to Scripture, is there actually such a thing as 'preaching' that can be differentiated in any way from other forms of word ministry? Or, if there *was* such a phenomenon in the context of the Old Testament prophetic ministries, or in the ministries of Jesus and his apostles, is there *still* such a thing as a specialized word ministry called 'preaching' in the post-apostolic age? After all, this is the age when the Spirit-filled company of believers are all empowered to speak God's word (see Acts 2:18, for instance). Perhaps preaching as a specialized activity is now completely outmoded. Most studies of preaching simply assume that there is an identifiable and specialized phenomenon called 'preaching' that continues in the post-apostolic age; but it seems necessary to address this question carefully from Scripture and not simply to accept this common assumption.

This discussion needs to be set firmly against the backdrop of Scripture's clear teaching that all God's people are called to be involved in word ministry. All believers have a part to play in the 'work of ministry, for building up the body of Christ' through 'speaking the truth in love' (Eph. 4:12, 15). As a whole people of God, we are to long and pray that 'the word of Christ' would dwell in us richly, so that we might be equipped for 'teaching and admonishing one another in all wisdom' (Col. 3:16). All believers are called to 'exhort' and 'encourage' one another in the word (Heb. 3:13; 10:25). Looking outward, the New Testament reflects both the historical reality that believers were involved in the evangelistic mission of the church, and the expectation that they should continue to be so involved.[3]

Given that the New Testament envisages a range of word ministries within the church, part of our task here is to discern how 'preaching' (if we can identify and define such a thing in the teaching of the NT) fits within the broader phenomenon of the ministry of the word in which all believers are rightly engaged. How does the pastor-teacher's 'preaching' relate to the word ministry of the small-group Bible-study leader, or of the believer who jots a note of Bible-based encouragement to a discouraged friend, or of the Christian who explains the gospel to her colleague at work?

[3] See the more detailed treatment of these points in chapter 3 below.

2

This issue has come to the fore in recent years in the context of the very healthy growth in every-member ministry in many churches. Much evangelicalism of an earlier age centred on the ministry of one person in a congregation. Fifty years ago, in many evangelical churches the senior minister would be expected to do more or less all the word ministry and pastoral care. Rightly, we have been learning more and more to encourage ministry by all God's people within the church family. Many larger churches have significant numbers of highly educated laypeople who are able and equipped to teach the Bible in a variety of settings, and so the standard of 'lay' word ministry is often very high. This is a cause for much thanksgiving, and we should pray that this trend might continue and increase in the years to come.

These healthy developments in our evangelical culture sharpen the question for us: If the saints are well equipped for the 'work of ministry' and are fruitfully 'speaking the truth in love' so that the body of Christ is built up (Eph. 4:12–15), can we really discern a difference between the word ministry of, say, a small-group Bible-study leader and that of the preacher on Sunday? Does Scripture establish a real theological distinction there? Or is a view that in any sense sets pulpit preaching apart from other forms of word ministry simply a carry-over from an earlier age of evangelicalism – a piece of historical and cultural baggage which has no real basis in Scripture and which is best discarded? To focus the question further: *According to Scripture, is there such a thing as 'preaching' that is mandated in the post-apostolic context; and, if there is, how is it characterized and defined?*

If we allow for a moment that according to Scripture there might be such a thing as 'preaching' in the post-apostolic context, we then encounter a second and related question: How would post-apostolic 'preaching' relate to the preaching of the Old Testament prophets and of Jesus and his apostles? As noted above, very few biblical or theological treatments of preaching demonstrate from Scripture that there is a line of continuity between those preaching ministries. Before attempting to learn anything about the nature of post-apostolic preaching from the ministries of the Old Testament prophets, Jesus or the apostles, it is important to consider carefully whether the New Testament establishes such a continuity, and, if so, what the nature of that continuity is.

To address these questions in any detail will require careful and extended analysis of a number of key New Testament texts. Because this study is focused particularly on these questions from the New Testament (and is not designed to attempt to exegete all parts of

Scripture that relate in some way to the question of preaching) it should be possible to devote more dedicated space to the analysis of these few key texts than has been possible in more wide-ranging studies.

Why these questions matter

Establishing whether there is a biblical basis for the practice of 'preaching' is vitally important because our conclusion on that matter will determine whether we cling on to preaching in times when it falls out of favour in evangelical culture or in seasons of church life when it appears to be less effective. If the significance of preaching is merely its historical pedigree or practical usefulness, then there is little compelling reason to maintain the practice of preaching when times change.

Clarifying the theological nature of preaching is similarly important because our conclusions will have significant effects on a number of aspects of our ministry and church life. They will inform how we relate other forms of word ministry to preaching; they will give shape to our preparation and delivery of sermons; they will inform how preachers pray for their preaching; and they will determine what congregations should rightly expect from preaching.

Finally, in churches that hold complementarian convictions concerning the roles of men and women in ministry, establishing the distinctive nature of preaching (if it is found to have one) will be an essential foundation to the discussion of whether or not it is appropriate for women to preach. Certainly, if we were to conclude that there was no distinctive theological character to preaching, it might then seem necessary for churches that allow only men to preach to revisit their position. Excluding women from one form of word ministry and not from another might be judged arbitrary and unjustified. Given the fact that the debate concerning gender roles in ministry is only intensifying and leading to increased division, it is all the more vital for churches to ensure that decisions about practice in this area are carefully grounded in Scripture.

The shape and scope of this study

The central interest of this book is to search the New Testament to address the questions articulated above. It will consist primarily of a series of exegetical studies of key New Testament texts that relate to preaching. But before turning to those exegetical studies, Part 1 will address three foundational matters. First among these is a brief biblical-theological overview of the theology of the word of God. If preaching is a ministry of the word, then its character will be shaped fundamentally by the character of the word itself. Thus an overview of a biblical theology of the word must set the foundation for any further theological conclusions we may reach about the nature of preaching. We will then turn to an overview of key Greek terms related to preaching in the New Testament, the findings of which will significantly inform our exegetical studies. A study of preaching in the New Testament will necessarily relate preaching to other ministries of the word within the life of the church, and so the third chapter will give attention to the New Testament's teaching concerning the scope and character of those varied ministries.

The exegetical studies in Part 2 will concentrate on sections of New Testament teaching that relate especially to the post-apostolic context. This naturally leads us to a particular focus on the later New Testament and particularly the epistles. In some epistles the activity of preaching in the post-apostolic context is directly in view (such as in 2 Timothy and Hebrews). In others, sections where Paul reflects upon (and defends) his own apostolic preaching ministry broaden out in various ways to bear upon the preaching of his non-apostolic associates and others, providing areas of fruitful exegetical reflection for us.

It will not be possible to take into account the full range of relevant material in the epistles in a study of this size, but we will focus on a number of epistles (and particular passages within the epistles) that relate most directly to the question of preaching. We will consider 2 Timothy 3 – 4 (with a particular focus on 4:2), where Paul charges Timothy to 'preach'; Romans 10, where Paul considers the commissioning of preachers and the role of preaching in the salvation purposes of God; 1 Corinthians (especially chs. 1–2, 9 and 15), where Paul defends his preaching ministry and methods at Corinth; 2 Corinthians (especially chs. 3–5), where Paul reflects upon the nature of new-covenant preaching ministry in relation to old-covenant ministry; 1 Thessalonians (especially chs. 1–2), where Paul reflects on his own preaching ministry and its fruit in Thessalonica; and Hebrews, which is itself a written sermon.

Finally, Part 3 will summarize the exegetical findings of the study and set them within the context of biblical theology, proposing a number of broader theological implications.

The length, scope and technical detail of this study are intentionally limited in order to make the work as accessible as possible. These limitations mean that it cannot claim to be an exhaustive exegetical and theological study of 'preaching' in the New Testament. It is, rather, a series of exegetical and theological observations from a number of key texts, with a view to addressing the questions outlined above. Any answers proposed to those questions are offered somewhat tentatively, knowing that there is certainly more exegetical work to be done in the New Testament in this area.

The level of close attention to the exegesis of certain New Testament texts required in order to carry out this investigation has necessitated some basic engagement with Greek semantics. Discussion of these matters has been framed in non-technical terms as far as possible, and Greek text has been transliterated where it has been necessary to include it. In general, the design and ambition of the investigation is to be sufficiently robust to be stimulating for those who have already given thought to the issues it addresses and who may have particular expertise in New Testament studies, as well as sufficiently accessible to be readable for pastors, whose time for study is so often limited.

Part I:
Foundational matters

Chapter One

The word of God
in biblical theology

This study will seek to set the New Testament's presentation of preaching within a wider biblical-theological framework. There can be little doubt that the primary biblical-theological category into which preaching falls is that of the word of God itself. If preaching is a ministry of the word, its character must be shaped fundamentally by the nature of the word itself. Thus our first task is to consider key features of the theological character of the word of God according to Scripture. This overview will not help us to distinguish preaching from other ministries of the word, but it will help us to see what preaching as one ministry of the word will involve and achieve. Although this overview will be brief and non-technical, it will serve an important function for this study. By establishing (or, for many readers, simply recapitulating) the broad parameters and characteristics of the word of God itself according to Scripture, we will be guarded from concluding that all the theological features we will find in the New Testament's presentation of preaching are unique to preaching. Indeed, we will find that many of the theological features of preaching in the New Testament's presentation are simply natural outworkings of the Bible's theology of the word of God itself.

God speaks through his word

Before issuing the well-known charge to Timothy to 'preach the word' (2 Tim. 4:2), Paul reminds him that the Bible is 'breathed out by God' (2 Tim. 3:16). Scripture has its origin directly in God such that the words of the Bible are God's words. However, the striking thing we discover as we look more broadly through Scripture to discern the theological character of the word is that God continues to speak today through the words that he once spoke. Scripture is not simply a depository and record of words that God spoke at some time in the past; it is the script that he continues to speak today. Scripture presents itself as a living thing.

9

We could turn to a number of places within Scripture to see this principle established and affirmed, but the handling of Old Testament Scripture in the book of Hebrews is particularly striking in this regard. The writer of Hebrews repeatedly treats Old Testament texts as being spoken by God in the contemporary context. So he can introduce quotations from psalms written centuries before with the words 'he [that is, God] says' (Heb. 1:6, 8). He adds more contemporary colour to a psalm quotation which is introduced as being the word of Jesus, saying that the words of the psalm reflect the feelings and disposition of Jesus: 'That is why he is not ashamed to call them brothers, saying, "I will tell of your name to my brothers"' (Heb. 2:11–12). He introduces words from another psalm by saying 'as the Holy Spirit says' (Heb. 3:7). God continues to speak the ancient words that he once spoke. That is why Hebrews refers to God's word as 'living and active' (Heb. 4:12).

This truth is vital for us to remember when it comes to any ministry of the word – and particularly when it comes to the ministry of preaching. If it is the word of God that preachers preach, then insofar as they are saying what the Bible passage is saying, it follows that God is speaking and his voice is heard. This truth may be so familiar that it has lost something of its wonder, but it is an extraordinary thing to consider. When preachers open up God's word and say what it says, God is speaking, and the congregation is hearing his own voice.

God acts through his word

Words are powerful things. It is easy to imagine that words are empty and action is all that counts. But the reality is that in speaking we are acting.[1] This is more obviously the case at some times than at others. Consider the words spoken by a man and woman at their wedding ceremony. As they say to each other, 'I . . . take you . . .', through those very words they become a married couple.[2] Through our words, though, we do things all the time: we reveal our hearts, we redefine relationships with others, we make commitments and we initiate

---

[1] This point was famously established by J. L. Austin's (1975) aptly named study on the philosophy of language and speech-act theory, *How to Do Things with Words*.

[2] The idea of a wedding ceremony as an example of effective speech comes from Dever and Gilbert 2012: 23, although the point can be traced back to Austin 1975: 5–6. I am grateful to Christopher Ash for his insight that it is the bride and groom's reciprocal words (rather than the minister's) that effect the marriage.

action. The writer of James dramatically points to the power of the tongue to bring about change: 'How great a forest is set ablaze by such a small fire! And the tongue is a fire, a world of unrighteousness' (Jas 3:5b–6a).

If human words are powerful, it stands to reason that God's words should be even more so. The principle that God's words issue forth in powerful action is established on the very first page of the Bible. In Genesis 1 God speaks the world into being. The repeated refrain of that chapter is simple but awe-inspiring: 'And God said . . . And there was . . .' The wonder of the fact that God spoke the world into being was not lost on the Old Testament people of God, but was a cause for reverent praise:

> By the word of the LORD the heavens were made,
> and by the breath of his mouth all their host . . .
> Let all the earth fear the LORD;
> let all the inhabitants of the world stand in awe of him!
> For he spoke, and it came to be;
> he commanded, and it stood firm.
>
> (Ps. 33:6, 8–9)

God not only created the good world by his word; he also brings healing to a broken world through his word. When the afflicted people of God cried out to him for help, 'He sent out his word and healed them, and delivered them from their destruction' (Ps. 107:20). When Ezekiel was taken to look upon the valley full of dry bones (picturing the people of God in exile and under the judgment of God), he was called to speak to them that they might live:

> So I prophesied as I was commanded. And as I prophesied, there was a sound, and behold, a rattling, and the bones came together, bone to its bone. And I looked, and behold, there were sinews on them, and flesh had come upon them, and skin had covered them . . . So I prophesied as he commanded me, and the breath came into them, and they lived and stood on their feet, an exceedingly great army. (Ezek. 37:7–10)

God by his word brought life to the dead in an act of re-creation hardly less dramatic or miraculous than his creative work in Genesis 1. With this same truth in his mind (and perhaps even remembering this very image) Peter could say to believers that 'you have been born again, not of perishable seed but of imperishable, through the living and abiding word of God' (1 Pet. 1:23).

However, there is another side to God's word. While it can bring salvation, it also effects God's judgment. To the false prophet who presumes to speak falsehood in his name, the Lord issues this warning and reminder: 'Is not my word like fire, declares the LORD, and like a hammer that breaks the rock in pieces?' (Jer. 23:29). Jesus warns that the words he speaks will judge those who hear them but fail to keep them:

> If anyone hears my words and does not keep them, I do not judge him; for I did not come to judge the world but to save the world. The one who rejects me and does not receive my words has a judge; the word that I have spoken will judge him on the last day. (John 12:47–48)

This judicial function of the word is reflected in the passage from Hebrews 4 quoted earlier: 'For the word of God is living and active, sharper than any two-edged sword, piercing to the division of soul and of spirit, of joints and of marrow, and discerning the thoughts and intentions of the heart' (Heb. 4:12). Ultimately, the judicial power of the word comes to full and dramatic expression in the final judgment, when the enemies of God are judged by Jesus through his word: 'From his mouth comes a sharp sword with which to strike down the nations, and he will rule them with a rod of iron' (Rev. 19:15). And so his enemies 'were slain by the sword that came from the mouth of him who was sitting on the horse, and all the birds were gorged with their flesh' (Rev. 19:21).

God's words are active; they always issue forth in God's action and do his work. By his word, God creates, rules, saves and judges. God's word is never empty or passive, but always achieves his work.

> For as the rain and the snow come down from heaven
>   and do not return there but water the earth,
> making it bring forth and sprout,
>   giving seed to the sower and bread to the eater,
> so shall my word be that goes out from my mouth;
>   it shall not return to me empty,
> but it shall accomplish that which I purpose,
>   and shall succeed in the thing for which I sent it.
>   (Isa. 55:10–11)

God is encountered in his word

As we have seen already, from the very first pages of Scripture God makes himself known as a speaking God. One of the great distinguishing marks of the God of the Bible as opposed to the mute idols of the nations is that God speaks (see Isa. 44:6–8). It is therefore unsurprising that God relates to his people primarily through his word. That truth is powerfully illustrated in the architecture of the tabernacle and, later, the temple. At the very centre of the place of meeting between God and his people, within the Most Holy Place, was the ark of the covenant, containing God's covenant word to his people on the tablets of the law.

Encounters with God in Scripture are often, in essence, encounters with his word. Even where a striking physical manifestation of God's presence is given, the substance of a meeting is verbal in nature. This is the case in God's meeting with Moses at the burning bush in Exodus 3. Although the burning bush catches Moses' attention (Exod. 3:3) and marks the fact that God is present, the essence of God's presence in the encounter is not so much the bush itself but the word that God speaks. Once God has Moses' attention, the substance of their encounter is a lengthy conversation (Exod. 3:7 – 4:17). The physical manifestation of God's presence only draws attention to the central means by which God engages with Moses: that is, by speaking to him.

The same is true for the prophet Elijah in his encounter with God in 1 Kings 19. Elijah is isolated and frightened, and in his goodness the Lord comes to him and makes his presence known to him. The encounter is dramatic, but once again God's word stands at the very heart of it:

> And he said, 'Go out and stand on the mount before the LORD.' And behold, the LORD passed by, and a great and strong wind tore the mountains and broke in pieces the rocks before the LORD, but the LORD was not in the wind. And after the wind an earthquake, but the LORD was not in the earthquake. And after the earthquake a fire, but the LORD was not in the fire. And after the fire the sound of a low whisper . . . And behold, there came a voice to him and said . . . (1 Kgs 19:11–13)

The striking physical manifestations of God's presence here again draw attention to the voice of God, which is the essence of the encounter.

Throughout Scripture God's identity and work are bound up in his word. The great development at the opening of the New Testament is that the word that was spoken through the ages and that has done the work of God throughout history is now enfleshed in the person of Jesus Christ:

> In the beginning was the Word, and the Word was with God, and the Word was God. He was in the beginning with God. All things were made through him, and without him was not any thing made that was made . . . And the Word became flesh and dwelt among us, and we have seen his glory, glory as of the only Son from the Father, full of grace and truth. (John 1:1–3, 14; see also Heb. 1:1–4)

Since Jesus is the Word made flesh, it is quite natural that he should place great emphasis on our hearing, responding to, and keeping the words that he goes on to speak. At the end of John's Gospel, as Jesus begins to prepare his disciples for the time when he will not be with them physically, he lays increasing emphasis on the centrality of the words that he speaks for relating to him. What he says in these final chapters is significant and worth pausing to consider in some detail.[3]

In John 14 Jesus makes it clear that in some measure he extends the unity that he shares with the Father to his disciples as well. Crucially, he sets his word (and their response to his word) at the heart of this relational dynamic:

> In that day [the day when Jesus departs] you will know that I am in my Father, and you in me, and I in you. Whoever has my commandments and keeps them, he it is who loves me. And he who loves me will be loved by my Father, and I will love him and manifest myself to him. (John 14:20–22)

In response to this, Judas asks how it is that Jesus will 'manifest' himself to his people (14:22). Jesus' reply sets the word at the centre again: 'If anyone loves me, he will keep my word, and my Father will love him, and we will come to him and make our home with him. Whoever does not love me does not keep my words' (14:23–24). The 'manifestation' of Jesus after his departure will be through his word.

---

[3] I am grateful to Rebecca Hollands, my former colleague at the Proclamation Trust, for drawing my attention to this section of John's Gospel and its relevance to the present discussion.

The response of the disciples to Jesus' word counts as a personal response to him, because Jesus is so intimately bound up in his word.

In chapter 15 Jesus seems to draw a close parallel between 'abiding in him' and his words 'abiding' in his disciples. These two types of 'abiding' are so closely related that they appear to be two sides of the same coin: 'Abide in me, and I in you . . . If you abide in me, *and my words abide in you*, ask whatever you wish, and it will be done for you' (John 15:4, 7, emphasis mine). Knowing Jesus and 'abiding' in him in true unity involves the word of Jesus 'abiding' in the believer by the power of the Spirit (see John 16:4–15). It is the Spirit who will take the words of Jesus (which he received from the Father) and declare them to the disciples (John 16:15). This encounter with God through his word is thoroughly Trinitarian. God the Father speaks his word; this word consists, in its fullness, in the Person of his Son, and it is mediated by the power of his Spirit. Thus the word as mediated by the Spirit is the central means by which the relationship between Jesus and the believer is established and maintained after the ascension.[4]

When Jesus prays for believers in John 17, he begins by telling the Father that he has faithfully made him (that is, the Father) known to the disciples:

> I have manifested your name [that is, your person and identity] to the people whom you gave me out of the world. Yours they were, and you gave them to me, and they have kept your word. Now they know that everything that you have given me is from you. For I have given them the words that you gave me, and they have received them and have come to know in truth that I came from you; and they have believed that you sent me. (17:6–8)

In giving his disciples the words that the Father gave him, Jesus has 'manifested' the Father to them. The disciples have, in turn, received those words. Ultimately, this means that they have received the Father and 'they are yours' (John 17:9).

Knowing and abiding in Jesus, and, through him, in the Father, happens as the word of Jesus is received and abides in those who hear. Jesus and the Father are 'manifested' through the word. This process continues beyond the earthly ministry of Jesus as his disciples speak his word: 'I do not ask for these only, but also for those who will

---

[4] On the integral interconnection between the word and the Spirit in John's Gospel, see Ash 2011. To set this observation within a broader doctrinal framework, see also Ward 2009: 78–95.

believe in me *through their word*, that they may all be one, just as you, Father, are in me, and I in you, that they also may be in us' (17:20–21, emphasis mine). As the disciples speak the word of Jesus after the time of the ascension, others will be able to enter into the unity that the people of God share with Jesus and the Father (see also 1 John 1:1–3, where this same dynamic is reflected).

Given the nature of the word as outlined here, we can conclude that at least three things must occur in and through any ministry of the word: (1) God is speaking, because through the Bible and by his Spirit God speaks today those words he once spoke; (2) God is achieving his purposes, because God's word is living and active; and (3) God is encountering his people, because he characteristically meets and relates to his people through his word. These features will be true of preaching as a ministry of the word, just as they will be true of any other ministry of the word. Nothing here sets preaching apart from any other form of word ministry, and so it remains to investigate whether there are distinctive theological features in the New Testament's portrayal of preaching.

Chapter Two

The language of 'preaching' in the New Testament

We cannot hope to develop a complete understanding of the New Testament's portrayal of preaching merely by studying the Greek vocabulary it uses in connection with the activity.[1] The possible pitfalls of word studies are well known,[2] and our aim here is not to construct a theological portrait of preaching based simply on a survey of relevant vocabulary. Nevertheless, it is equally true that an understanding of the key vocabulary and its use in the New Testament is a necessary foundation for this study.

There are quite a number of Greek verbs used in connection with the transmission or communication of God's word or the gospel in the New Testament, but our particular interest is in the distinctive characteristics of *preaching* as a ministry of the word. Therefore we will limit ourselves to a consideration of the key verbs that appear to be used to refer specifically to the activity of preaching.[3] That limitation naturally raises the question (in many ways the basic question of this study): What is preaching? A final answer to that question will have to wait until the conclusion of this book but, for the purposes of the discussion that follows in this chapter, a working definition of 'preaching' is needed, and we will use the following: _preaching is a public proclamation of God's word_.

In her recent study of the vocabulary used in connection with the activity of teaching within four Pauline epistles (1 Corinthians, 1 and 2 Timothy, and Titus), Claire Smith has convincingly identified three verbs that function within that literature as 'semi-technical terms for gospel proclamation': *euangelizomai, katangellō* and *kēryssō*.[4] These

---

[1] So, rightly, Meyer 2013: 14, 316–317; Adam 1996: 75. Word studies are undoubtedly of value in considering the NT's conception of preaching, and a number have been undertaken (see e.g. Stott 1961 and Runia 1978: 3–48, esp. 7–20).

[2] See James Barr's (1961) frequently cited and foundational study.

[3] Again, there could be merit in widening the scope of the investigation to consider the various cognates of these verbs and so treat whole 'word groups', but we will not attempt to do so here.

[4] Smith 2012: 202.

three verbs are usually translated 'preach' or 'proclaim' in English versions of the New Testament (or, in the case of *euangelizomai*, 'preach good news' or 'proclaim good news'), and that is normally their natural and plain meaning. That much could probably not be said of any other verbs used in the New Testament. We will focus primarily on a consideration of these three key 'semi-technical' verbs identified by Smith, but will broaden the scope of the inquiry from her target literature to include the whole New Testament.

Before turning to give detailed attention to those three verbs, it is worth considering much more briefly two other verbs, *apangellō* and *martyreō*, which are sometimes used in relation to preaching in the New Testament but which would not normally be translated 'to preach'.[5] The verb *apangellō* occurs forty-six times in the New Testament[6] (primarily in the Gospels and Acts) and means to 'announce', 'report' or 'proclaim'.[7] In the New Testament it generally refers to the straightforward relaying of events or information, often of quite a mundane nature. Occasionally it refers to a 'proclamatory' reporting of significant salvific events centred on the life, death and resurrection of Jesus (see Acts 26:20; Heb. 2:12; 1 John 1:2, 3). In such cases, the choice of the verb *apangellō* to refer to a 'proclamation' lays emphasis on the speaker as an eyewitness with a responsibility, desire or compulsion to attest to the events or realities he conveys.

The verb *martyreō* occurs seventy-seven times in the New Testament[8] and means to 'bear witness' or 'testify' to a reality or event, or to the character of a person.[9] *Martyreō* is of interest because it is a favourite term for referring to the proclamatory ministry of Jesus in John's Gospel, a book which makes almost no use of the 'semi-technical' proclamatory terms we will consider below. This lexical choice on the part of the author resonates with an important

---

[5] Smith (2012: 202) classifies these two verbs as 'announcing' verbs alongside *euangelizomai*, *katangellō* and *kēryssō*, but rightly does not classify them as 'semi-technical terms for gospel proclamation'.
[6] Matt. 2:8; 8:33; 11:4; 12:18; 14:12; 28:8, 10, 11; Mark 5:14, 19; 6:30; 16:10, 13; Luke 7:18, 22; 8:20, 34, 36, 47; 9:36; 13:1; 14:21; 18:37; 24:9; John 16:25; Acts 4:23; 5:22, 25; 11:13; 12:14, 17; 15:27; 16:36, 38; 17:30; 22:26; 23:16, 17, 19; 26:20; 28:21; 1 Cor. 14:24; 1 Thess. 1:9; Heb. 2:12; 1 John 1:2, 3.
[7] See BDAG.
[8] Matt. 23:31; Luke 4:22; John 1:7, 8, 15, 32, 34; 2:25; 3:11, 26, 28, 32; 4:39, 44; 5:31, 32 (twice), 33, 36, 37, 39; 7:7; 8:13, 14, 18 (twice); 10:25; 12:17; 13:21; 15:26, 27; 18:23, 37; 19:35; 21:24; Acts 6:3; 10:22, 43; 13:22; 14:3; 15:8; 16:2; 22:5, 12; 23:11; 26:5, 22; Rom. 3:21; 10:2; 1 Cor. 15:15; 2 Cor. 8:3; Gal. 4:15; Col. 4:13; 1 Tim. 5:10; 6:13; Heb. 7:8, 17; 10:15; 11:2, 4 (twice), 5, 39; 1 John 1:2; 4:14; 5:6, 7, 9, 10; 3 John 3, 6, 12 (twice); Rev. 1:2; 22:16, 18, 20.
[9] See BDAG.

theme of John's Gospel, that is, Jesus as the Son who came from the Father, who bears faithful witness to the Father, and who speaks the words the Father gave him to speak. Arguably *martyreō* refers to Jesus' preaching activity on a number of occasions in John's Gospel, but it would generally not be natural to translate it 'preach' or 'proclaim'.

These two verbs are sometimes used in the New Testament to refer to gospel proclamation of the kind that we might class as 'preaching', in order to emphasize the character of that proclamation as 'reporting' (in the case of *apangellō*) or 'bearing witness' (in the case of *martureō*). However, clearly they are not 'semi-technical terms for gospel proclamation',[10] and they do not mean 'to preach'.

We turn now to consider in more detail the three verbs (*euangelizomai, katangellō* and *kēryssō*) that are the central focus of our interest. Smith has demonstrated that these three verbs (as they occur in her target literature) are used to denote didactic activity within the Pauline communities, and, in particular, the didactic activity of 'proclaiming' the gospel.[11] Our interest is to probe further and consider the particular and defining characteristics of these verbs and the activities to which they refer throughout the New Testament. How does the activity of 'proclaiming' fit within the broader matrix of didactic activities that took place within the early church, and how is it distinguishable from other didactic activities?

These concerns lead us to ask particular questions concerning each occurrence of these verbs in the New Testament: First, who is the speaker (or implied speaker)? Are particular individuals or groups the normal subjects of these verbs? Second, what is the context (or implied context) of the address? In particular, is it the case that these announcing verbs normally refer to a public address, or can they be used to refer to private and informal communication? Third, what can we discern of the content of the address? Once we have considered the basic lexical characteristics of each verb, we will outline data related to those three questions in chart form, and then summarize our findings for each verb individually. At the end of the chapter we will draw together these findings to propose some broader lexical conclusions.

---

[10] See Smith 2012: 202.
[11] Smith 2012: 163–205.

Euangelizomai

The verb *euangelizomai* occurs fifty-four times in the New Testament and means 'bring good news', 'announce good news' or 'proclaim the gospel'.[12] Its use in LXX Isaiah 52:7 and 61:1 (to refer to the activity of the messenger who announces the Lord's universal kingship and restoration of Zion) is a significant textual and theological foundation for its use within the New Testament to refer to the proclamation of the good news in Christ.[13] The related noun *euangelion* ('good news') can function as a verbal noun referring to the activity of proclamation,[14] but normally serves in the New Testament as a shorthand for the message of Christ's death and resurrection that is proclaimed.[15] It is perhaps natural, then, that the verb *euangelizomai* should generally import a particular emphasis on the content of the message (the 'good news') that is communicated.[16]

The following table outlines basic details concerning each occurrence of *euangelizomai* in the New Testament.

Reference	Speaker (or implied speaker)	Context (or implied context)	Content (or implied content)
Matt. 11:5	Jesus	public ministry of Jesus	good news for the poor
Luke 1:19	angel Gabriel	privately to Zechariah	John is to be born to Zechariah and Elizabeth; he will make people ready for the Lord
Luke 2:10	an angel of the Lord	shepherds	Christ the Lord is born
Luke 3:18	John the Baptist	the region around the Jordan	the coming of Christ
Luke 4:18	Jesus / anointed preacher of Isa. 61	synagogue in Nazareth initially, but referring to full scope of Jesus' ministry	good news to the poor, release, healing, the Lord's favour (that is, the gospel)
Luke 4:43	Jesus	'other towns'	'the kingdom of God'

[12] BDAG.
[13] O'Brien 1993: 79–80; TDNT 2.708–709.
[14] Smith 2012: 179.
[15] O'Brien 1993: 78, 80; Mitchell 1994: 63–68.
[16] Runia 1978: 19.

Reference	Speaker (or implied speaker)	Context (or implied context)	Content (or implied content)
Luke 7:22	Jesus	public ministry of Jesus	good news for the poor
Luke 8:1	Jesus	cities and villages	'the kingdom of God'
Luke 9:6	the Twelve	the villages	the gospel
Luke 16:16	implicitly Jesus (and possibly the Twelve)	not specified	'the kingdom of God'
Luke 20:1	Jesus	the temple	the gospel
Acts 5:42	the apostles	'in the temple and from house to house'	'Jesus as the Christ'
Acts 8:4	scattered believers	throughout Judea and Samaria	'the word'
Acts 8:12	Philip	the city of Samaria	'the kingdom of God and the name of Jesus Christ'
Acts 8:25	Peter and John	'many villages of the Samaritans'	the gospel
Acts 8:35	Philip	with the Ethiopian eunuch	'the good news about Jesus'
Acts 8:40	Philip	'all the towns' as he passed through Azotus on the way to Caesarea	the gospel
Acts 10:36	Jesus	Israel	'good news of peace'
Acts 11:20	scattered believers; 'men of Cyprus and Cyrene'	unspecified	'the Lord Jesus'
Acts 13:32	Paul (and possibly Barnabas)	synagogue at Antioch in Pisidia	the fulfilment of God's promises to the 'fathers' in Jesus and his resurrection
Acts 14:7	Paul and Barnabas	Lystra and Derbe	the gospel
Acts 14:15	Paul and Barnabas	Lystra	'that you should turn from these vain things to a living God'
Acts 14:21	Paul and Barnabas	Derbe	the gospel

Reference	Speaker (or implied speaker)	Context (or implied context)	Content (or implied content)
Acts 15:35	Paul and Barnabas 'with many others'	Antioch	'the word of the Lord'
Acts 16:10	Paul, Silas and Timothy (and Luke?)	Macedonia	the gospel
Acts 17:18	Paul	various locations in Athens, including the synagogue and the marketplace	Jesus and the resurrection
Rom. 1:15	Paul	the believers in Rome	the gospel
Rom. 10:15	someone who is sent to preach	not specified	Christ, the gospel
Rom. 15:20	Paul	where Christ has not 'already been named'	the gospel
1 Cor. 1:17	Paul	Corinth	the gospel
1 Cor. 9:16 (twice)	Paul	not specified	the gospel
1 Cor. 9:18	Paul	not specified	the gospel
1 Cor. 15:1	Paul	in Corinth, to those who came to faith	the gospel
1 Cor. 15:2	Paul	in Corinth, to those who came to faith	the gospel
2 Cor. 10:16	Paul (and possibly Timothy)	lands beyond Corinth	the gospel
2 Cor. 11:7	Paul	the church at Corinth	the gospel
Gal. 1:8	Paul 'or an angel from heaven'	the church at Galatia	a different 'gospel'
Gal. 1:8	Paul	the church at Galatia (with reference to earlier/ initial proclamation there)	the gospel
Gal. 1:9	any false teacher	the church at Galatia	'a gospel contrary to the one you received'
Gal. 1:11	Paul	Paul's ministry in general, perhaps with particular reference to Galatia	the gospel

Reference	Speaker (or implied speaker)	Context (or implied context)	Content (or implied content)
Gal. 1:16	Paul	'among the Gentiles'	God's Son
Gal. 1:23	Paul	unspecified; a reference to his broader ministry	'the faith'
Gal. 4:13	Paul	initial ministry in Galatia	the gospel
Eph. 2:17	Jesus	unspecified; preaching addressed to 'you who were far off' and 'those who were near'	'peace'
Eph. 3:8	Paul	Paul's broader ministry 'to the Gentiles'	'the unsearchable riches of Christ'
1 Thess. 3:6	Timothy	to Paul and Silas	news of the Thessalonians' 'faith and love'
Heb. 4:2	unspecified[17]	proclamation to the wilderness generation and to the believers addressed in Hebrews	good news
Heb. 4:6	unspecified	proclamation to the wilderness generation	good news
1 Pet. 1:12	unspecified	unspecified, but presumably the initial proclamation to the 'elect exiles of the dispersion' addressed in 1 Peter (see 1:1)	good news

[17] Arguably Hebrews here recalls Joshua and Caleb's proclamation of the goodness of the land and the continued opportunity (in line with the Abrahamic promise) of entering it, as recorded in Numbers 13 and 14 (Griffiths 2014: 69–73). In that case, the implied speakers are Joshua and Caleb at Heb. 4:2 and 4:6, and the implied context is 'all the congregation of the people of Israel in the wilderness of Paran, at Kadesh' (Num. 13:26).

Reference	Speaker (or implied speaker)	Context (or implied context)	Content (or implied content)
1 Pet. 1:25	unspecified	unspecified, but presumably the initial proclamation to the 'elect exiles of the dispersion' addressed in 1 Peter (see 1:1)	good news, the word of God
1 Pet. 4:6	unspecified	'to those who are dead'	the gospel
Rev. 10:7	God	to the prophets	the fulfilment of the 'mystery of God'
Rev. 14:6	an angel	'flying overhead', addressing the whole population of the earth	a call to 'fear God and give him glory' in light of coming judgment

A few observations can be made from the data outlined above. First, the agent of the communication is usually a figure of recognized authority: John the Baptist, Jesus, an apostle (or apostolic associate), an angel, or God himself. However, this is not always so. On two occasions in Acts, the speakers are unnamed scattered believers (Acts 8:4 and 11:20), and on some occasions the speakers are not explicitly identified (Heb. 4:2, 6; 1 Pet. 1:12, 25; 4:6).[18]

The context in which the speaking takes place is not always specified and, where it is specified, is somewhat variable. In general, a public context of some kind (often a synagogue) is identified or assumed. However, at Luke 1:19 the communication is made in private to one person, and at Acts 8:35 the communication is again directed to an individual. At Acts 5:42 the communication takes place both in the public context of the temple and in private homes.

Almost without exception, the substance of the communication is the gospel message or some particular aspect of it. This is evident either implicitly, where no object or description of the message is supplied and the plain meaning is 'proclaim good news' (as is frequently the case for *euangelizomai*),[19] or explicitly, where a description of the message is supplied. The single exception to this

[18] But see note above concerning Heb. 4:2, 6.
[19] In such cases we have recorded 'the gospel' as the substance of the message on the chart.

24

is 1 Thessalonians 3:6, where the 'good news' is a report of the Thessalonian believers' 'faith and love', rather than the gospel message about Christ.

Katangellō

The verb *katangellō* means to 'proclaim' or 'announce' and occurs eighteen times in the New Testament, as outlined in the following table.[20]

Reference	Speaker (or implied speaker)	Context (or implied context)	Content (or implied content)
Acts 3:24	The OT prophets	OT Israel	the days of fulfilment in Christ
Acts 4:2	Peter and John	Solomon's Portico	'in Jesus the resurrection from the dead'
Acts 13:5	Barnabas and Saul (with John?)	synagogues in Salamis	'the word of God'
Acts 13:38	Paul	synagogue at Antioch in Pisidia	'forgiveness of sins' through Jesus
Acts 15:36	Paul and Barnabas	various cities	'the word of the Lord'
Acts 16:17	Paul and Silas (and other companions)[21]	not specified	'the way of salvation'
Acts 16:21	Paul and Silas	unspecified public locations in Philippi	allegedly, 'customs that are not lawful for us as Romans to accept or practise'
Acts 17:3	Paul	synagogue in Thessalonica	that it was necessary for the Christ to suffer and rise; that Jesus is the Christ
Acts 17:13	Paul	synagogue in Berea	'the word of God'
Acts 17:23	Paul	Areopagus in Athens	'what . . . you worship as unknown'; the true God

[20] BDAG.

[21] On the question of whether the use of the first person plural in this section of the narrative indicates that Luke was present, see discussion in Peterson 2009: 456.

Reference	Speaker (or implied speaker)	Context (or implied context)	Content (or implied content)
Acts 26:23	Jesus	unspecified location post-resurrection; to Jews and Gentiles	'light'
Rom. 1:8	unspecified	'in all the world'	the faith of the Roman Christians
1 Cor. 2:1	Paul	unspecified locations in Corinth (but see Acts 18:1–11)	'the testimony of God'
1 Cor. 9:14	Paul (and others who should rightly 'get their living by the gospel')	not specified	'the gospel'
1 Cor. 11:26	those who partake of the Lord's Supper	the church gathered for the Lord's Supper	'the Lord's death until he comes'
Phil. 1:17	unspecified rivals of Paul's	unspecified	'Christ'
Phil. 1:18	unspecified[22]	unspecified	'Christ'
Col. 1:28	Paul (and possibly Timothy)	unspecified; a general reference to Paul's ministry of proclamation	Christ

This outline of the data shows a pattern of use in the New Testament for *katangellō* similar to that seen previously for *euangelizomai*. The speaker is normally a figure of recognized authority (usually an apostle, most frequently Paul). Where it is specified, the context of the proclamation is often a public venue, most frequently a synagogue. However, on a number of occasions, the context simply indicates that the proclamation took place in a particular town and no further detail is supplied, and on a few occasions the text gives no indication of the context of the proclamation. The subject matter is usually Christ and the gospel.

A few instances of the verb's use stand out as exceptional and merit comment.[23] In Romans 1:8 the substance of the proclamation is not the gospel, but the faith demonstrated by the Roman believers,

---

[22] See Excursus 1 for discussion of the identity of the speaker(s) in Phil. 1:17–18.

[23] Note also Phil. 1:17–18, where the agents of the proclamation are not named, and their identity is disputed. See Excursus 1 for detailed discussion.

and the speakers are unidentified. In this case, the term *katangellō* plainly does not mean 'preach'. The most striking exception to the pattern of use of *katangellō* is its use in 1 Corinthians 11:26 to refer to a corporate 'proclamation' of the Lord's death by the believers gathered for the Lord's Supper. Here the agents of the proclamation are clearly not specifically figures of authority. Their message centres on Christ and the gospel, but it is not even clear that their proclamation is verbal. Although the proclamation might be verbal, it is entirely possible that the 'proclamation' is simply the act of participating in the Supper. This use of the verb to specify a corporate proclamation, and one that is potentially 'enacted' rather than verbal, is noteworthy for its uniqueness.

Kēryssō

Possible translations for *kēryssō* include 'to announce', 'make known', 'proclaim aloud' and 'make proclamation as a herald'.[24] In the classical world, the *kēryx* was the herald of the king or the court, who had the dignified role ('partaking of the character of *an ambassador*', LS) of making public proclamations on the behalf of the monarch.[25] The cognate noun *kērygma* can refer either to the content of the proclamation or to the act of proclamation.[26] The verb *kēryssō* is used fifty-nine times in the New Testament, as outlined in the following table.

Reference	Speaker (or implied speaker)	Context (or implied context)	Content (or implied content)
Matt. 3:1	John the Baptist	the wilderness of Judea	'Repent, for the kingdom of heaven is at hand.'
Matt. 4:17	Jesus	initially Capernaum, but probably more general reference to his public ministry	'Repent, for the kingdom of heaven is at hand.'

[24] See BDAG and LS.
[25] LS also notes that another Classical use of the term *kēryx* is to refer to 'a prickly instrument of torture'. That meaning is, I trust, far removed from readers' conceptions and experiences of the preacher as *kēryx*!
[26] *Contra* Dodd 1936: 7–35, and many interpreters who followed him, who maintained that *kērygma* referred only to the content of the proclamation. '[T]he connotation of the word is such that, even when content is to the fore, it is nevertheless content that is to be made known through proclamation' (Smith 2012: 172). See also the substantial discussion in Litfin 2015: 195–213 as well as Grumm 1970: 178; McDonald 1980: 1–2; and Edsall 2014: 2–4.

Reference	Speaker (or implied speaker)	Context (or implied context)	Content (or implied content)
Matt. 4:23	Jesus	throughout Galilee; particularly in the synagogues	the gospel of the kingdom
Matt. 9:35	Jesus	the cities and villages of Israel, particularly in the synagogues	the gospel of the kingdom
Matt. 10:7	the Twelve	Israel ('to the lost sheep of the house of Israel')	'The kingdom of heaven is at hand'
Matt. 10:27	the Twelve	'on the housetops' (of the towns of Israel, see 10:5–6, 23)	not specified; presumably the gospel and its implications[27]
Matt. 11:1	Jesus	the cities of Israel	general teaching, gospel
Matt. 24:14	not specified, but implied as disciples (likely as contrast to false prophets: see 24:11)	throughout the whole world	the gospel of the kingdom
Matt. 26:13	not specified	throughout the whole world	'this gospel' (perhaps with particular reference to the message of Jesus' death (see 26:12)
Mark 1:4	John the Baptist	the wilderness of Judea	a baptism of repentance
Mark 1:7	John the Baptist	the wilderness of Judea	the coming of Jesus
Mark 1:14	Jesus	Galilee	the gospel of God
Mark 1:38	Jesus	towns in Galilee	general teaching, gospel
Mark 1:39	Jesus	synagogues in towns throughout Galilee	general teaching, gospel
Mark 1:45	cleansed leper	throughout Galilee	news of Jesus' healing of him
Mark 3:14	the Twelve	not specified; to be sent out	not specified; general teaching, gospel

[27] So Carson 1995: 254.

Reference	Speaker (or implied speaker)	Context (or implied context)	Content (or implied content)
Mark 5:20	healed demoniac	the Decapolis	what Jesus had done for him
Mark 6:12	the Twelve	Galilee	that people should repent
Mark 7:36	witnesses of a healing miracle	the Decapolis	that Jesus had healed the deaf man
Mark 13:10	implied as disciples	all nations	the gospel
Mark 14:9	not specified	the whole world	the gospel
Luke 3:3	John the Baptist	all the region around the Jordan	a baptism of repentance for the forgiveness of sins
Luke 4:18	Jesus / anointed preacher of Isa. 61	synagogue in Nazareth initially, but referring to full scope of Jesus' ministry	good news to the poor, release, healing, the Lord's favour (that is, the gospel)
Luke 4:19	as above		
Luke 4:44	Jesus	the synagogues of Judea	the good news of the kingdom of God
Luke 8:1	Jesus	cities and villages	the good news of the kingdom of God
Luke 8:39	healed demoniac	throughout the whole city (a city of the Gerasenes)	how much Jesus had done for him
Luke 9:2	the Twelve	throughout the villages	the kingdom of God
Luke 12:3	not specified, but probably implied as God (in his ultimate work of judgment)	'the housetops'	acts that are currently hidden but will be disclosed in the judgment[28]
Luke 24:47	not specified, but implied as apostles/ disciples (see 24:48)	all nations	repentance and forgiveness of sins
Acts 8:5	Philip	the city of Samaria; the crowds (see 8:6)	the Christ
Acts 9:20	Saul	the synagogues of Damascus	Jesus; that 'He is the Son of God'

[28] See further discussion in Bock 1994: 221–222.

Reference	Speaker (or implied speaker)	Context (or implied context)	Content (or implied content)
Acts 10:37	John the Baptist	implied context is John's public ministry in Judea	John's baptism
Acts 10:42	Peter and the other apostles (as commissioned by Jesus)	'to the people'	not specified precisely, but 10:39–43 indicates it is the gospel message, as witnesses of Jesus
Acts 15:21	Jewish leaders/ teachers who speak in the synagogues	Jewish synagogue	'Moses'
Acts 19:13	Paul	not specified, but Paul's public ministry is implied	Jesus
Acts 20:25	Paul	referring to his ministry in Ephesus	the kingdom
Acts 28:31	Paul	referring to his ministry in Rome while under house arrest	the kingdom of God
Rom. 2:21	the Jews	not specified; implies public ethical instruction/ exhortation	against stealing
Rom. 10:8	'we': Paul (and others who preach?)	not specified	'the word of faith that we proclaim'; that Jesus is Lord and that God raised him from the dead (see 10:9)
Rom. 10:14	someone who is sent to preach	not specified; the context indicates a 'hearing'	Christ, the gospel
Rom. 10:15	someone who is sent to preach	not specified; the context indicates a 'hearing'	Christ, the gospel
1 Cor. 1:23	Paul	to Jews and Greeks	Christ crucified
1 Cor. 9:27	Paul	not specified; general preaching ministry 'to others'	not specified; general preaching of the gospel

Reference	Speaker (or implied speaker)	Context (or implied context)	Content (or implied content)
1 Cor. 15:11	Paul and the apostles	proclamation to the Corinthians	Christ, his death and resurrection
1 Cor. 15:12	Paul and the apostles	proclamation to the Corinthians	the resurrection of Christ
2 Cor. 1:19	Paul, Silas and Timothy	proclamation to the Corinthians	the Son of God, Jesus Christ
2 Cor. 4:5	Paul (presumably Silas and Timothy as well)	ministry of proclamation to the Corinthians	Jesus Christ as Lord
2 Cor. 11:4 (twice)	Paul and false apostles	proclamation to the Corinthians	Jesus (as proclaimed by Paul vs. as proclaimed by false apostles)
Gal. 2:2	Paul	'among the Gentiles'	the gospel
Gal. 5:11	Paul	general preaching ministry	the content of his message (the cross, not circumcision)
Phil. 1:15	unspecified rivals and allies of Paul[29]	not specified	Christ
Col. 1:23	not specified; but at least Paul in part	'in all creation under heaven'	the gospel
1 Thess. 2:9	Paul, probably with Silas and Timothy	ministry in Thessalonica	the gospel of God
1 Tim. 3:16	not specified	'among the nations'	Christ
2 Tim. 4:2	Timothy	to the church in Ephesus (in the first instance)	'the word'
1 Pet. 3:19	Christ, in the Spirit	'the spirits in prison'	not specified
Rev. 5:2	an angel	by the heavenly throne; to those in heaven and earth	'Who is worthy to open the scroll and break its seals?'

As this table makes clear, in the vast majority of cases where *kēryssō* is used, the agent of the proclamation is a person of recognized authority (John the Baptist, Jesus, an apostle or an apostolic agent). Occasionally the speaker is not specified. There are a few occasions when a person who lacks recognized authority makes a

---

[29] See Excursus 1 for discussion concerning the identity of the speaker(s).

public proclamation; in particular, there are three instances in Mark (with one parallel incident in Luke) where a person who has been healed, or some witnesses to a healing, go and make public proclamation of what Jesus has done (Mark 1:45; 5:20/Luke 8:39; Mark 7:36). However, in each of these cases Jesus gives instruction that the healed person should go home or to the priests at the temple to tell (but not 'proclaim') what he has done, but in each case the text makes it quite clear that the person or people involved go beyond what they are told to do (arguably in acts of disobedience) in making a proclamation.

These observations resonate with the New Testament's use of the cognate terms *kēryx* (meaning 'herald' or 'preacher') and *kērygma* (meaning 'preaching' or 'preached message'). The term *kēryx* occurs three times in the New Testament, on each occasion referring to an authoritative agent of divine communication. Twice Paul refers to his appointment as a *kēryx* alongside reference to his appointment as 'apostle' and 'teacher' (1 Tim. 2:7; 2 Tim. 1:11), and on one occasion Peter refers to Noah as a 'preacher [*kēryx*] of righteousness' (2 Pet. 2:5, NIV). The term *kērygma* in the New Testament refers to the 'preaching' or 'preached message' of Paul on every occasion it is used (Rom. 16:25; 1 Cor. 1:21; 2:4; 15:14; 2 Tim. 4:17; Titus 1:3), save for one instance in the Synoptics, where it refers to the preaching of Jonah (Matt. 12:41/Luke 11:32).

To return to the use of *kēryssō* throughout the New Testament, in the vast majority of these instances the context of the proclamation is a public one (a town or a city, a synagogue, or even the whole world). The case of Paul's proclamation of the gospel while under house arrest in Rome (Acts 28:31), which may have involved people coming to hear him speak in the house where he was held (or, given the rather relaxed nature of that imprisonment, could conceivably have involved his speaking in another venue), is ambiguous and is possibly an exception to the pattern. If we set aside this one somewhat ambiguous instance, there is no other instance where *kēryssō* is used to designate private communication at the level of a conversation between individuals.[30]

Almost uniformly, the substance of the message proclaimed where *kēryssō* is used is the gospel message and its implications (or, more broadly, the teaching of or about Jesus).

---

[30] Even where Paul's house arrest is concerned, the 'preaching' in Acts 28 forms part of the public ministry of one who is (by that time) a public figure and a person of recognized authority within the church.

Summary, conclusions and further reflections

1. The observations of this chapter confirm that *euangelizomāi, katangellō* and *kēryssō* do function with a high degree of consistency as 'semi-technical' terms for preaching the gospel throughout the New Testament. The designation '*semi*-technical' is apt because there is some variety in use, and it is not the case that every occurrence of the vocabulary is a 'technical' reference to preaching (unless the definition of preaching is made very broad indeed). It is important to recognize the distinction between words and the concepts to which they point.[31] Purely 'technical' terms refer precisely and uniformly to a specific and closely defined concept within a body of literature. These three verbs are rightly classified as 'semi-technical' because they appear frequently to refer to a particular concept: that of preaching. As used in the New Testament, the verbs typically refer to the act of making a public proclamation;[32] the agent is generally a person of recognized authority; and the substance of the proclamation is normally some aspect of Christ's Person and work, the implications of the gospel, or some other truth from God's word. There are, as we have noted, exceptions to this pattern of use, but the frequency of occurrence of the terms, the range of documents across which they appear and the high degree of consistency in meaning are striking features of their use and confirm the appropriateness of designating the terms as 'semi-technical' in nature. Furthermore, the fact that the New Testament regularly uses this group of verbs in a specialized way to refer to the public proclamation of God's word/the gospel by a leader strongly

---

[31] Barr 1961: 207.

[32] To speak of preaching as a 'public' activity is not to claim that it happened exclusively in typical 'public' venues such as the gymnasium or even the street corner. Stowers (1984: 59–82) has sought to argue that the most important venue for Paul's preaching was the household, meaning that his preaching was set in a 'private' context rather than a 'public' one. The distinction is partly just semantic, resting on a particular definition of 'public' and 'private'. Whatever definition is adopted for those terms, however, Stowers' point seems strained. As he himself notes, much education in the Graeco-Roman world took place in the home, which 'seems to have been the most popular place for philosophers and sophists to hold their classes' (66). As far as the early churches were concerned, the house churches 'are clearly the focus of community life in Paul's letters' (65), and it seems clear from passages such as 1 Cor. 14 that 'non-believers were invited into homes even for the worship of the assembled church' (69). If we allow for a definition of a 'public' context as encompassing any context where a group of people would gather to hear a speaker, surely a gathering in a home would qualify. Indeed, in the modern-day context, where many house churches and new church plants gather in homes to hear the preaching of God's word, such a situation is once again familiar and quite normal.

suggests that we are justified in speaking of 'preaching' as a recognized and distinct activity in the New Testament.

2. Previous analyses of the vocabulary associated with gospel proclamation in the New Testament have proposed distinctions between language that is used in association with evangelistic proclamation and language used in association with the edification of believers.[33] We have not attempted to examine in detail the question of the faith status of the addressees of the 'proclamations' referred to using the three key verbs. However, from the general observations outlined above, it is unquestionably the case that the bulk of the occurrences of the three 'semi-technical' verbs are found in the context of evangelistic proclamation to non-Christians. This is no surprise given that the New Testament book with the most frequent occurrences of the vocabulary is Acts, which is dominated by accounts of pioneer evangelism. Many of the other occurrences of the vocabulary are in sections of Paul's epistles where he is recounting his earlier (often initial) ministry in a given place, again suggesting that the proclamation he refers to addressed non-Christians in the first instance. Again, this is no great surprise. Much of the New Testament either describes (throughout the Gospels and Acts) or recalls (at various points in the epistles) evangelistic outreach, so it stands to reason that a significant proportion of the occurrences of terms associated with proclamation will refer to evangelistic proclamation of the gospel.

However, a number of instances of the key terms do occur in contexts where the edification of believers appears to be in view, and these occurrences caution us against concluding that the New Testament establishes a clear-cut distinction between gospel proclamation to unbelievers and gospel proclamation to believers. At Romans 1:15, addressing believers within an established church (see 1:7), Paul writes, 'I am eager to preach the gospel [euangelisasthai] to you also who are in Rome.'[34] Paul's insistence that the believers in Corinth bear

---

[33] Most famously, Dodd 1936: 7–35. See also Dickson 2005: 212–230.

[34] Alternative interpretations of Rom. 1:15 have been proposed. Dickson (2005: 223–230) has argued that Paul's reference here is retrospective, and he means that he wished he had been the one to make the initial proclamation of the gospel at Rome. Evans (1981: 317–318) has proposed that the 'good news' Paul longed to share was the progress of his own ministry, rather than the gospel message. According to Evans, '[t]he fact that Paul mentions the gospel in the following verse means no more than that the verb brought to mind the noun euangelion'. On the contrary, the use of the noun euangelion in Rom. 1:16 with clear reference to the gospel message strongly suggests that Paul's reference to 'preaching the good news' in the previous verse does indeed refer to what it appears to refer to, namely, 'preaching the gospel'. Neither of these

a responsibility for supporting those who engage in gospel proclamation (1 Cor. 9:14) suggests that the believers themselves benefited from that ministry of proclamation as hearers.[35] In Colossians 1:28 Paul summarizes his ministry (and that of his ministry associates) in this way: 'Him we proclaim [*katangellomen*], warning everyone and teaching everyone with all wisdom, that we may present everyone mature in Christ.' The language of 'warning' and 'teaching' sheds light on the nature of Paul's 'proclamation', making it quite clear that it 'describes not simply the initial apostolic announcement, but draws attention to the ongoing and systematic presentation of Christ as Lord as well'.[36] The charge of 2 Timothy 4:2 (to which we will give detailed attention below) to 'preach [*kēryxon*] the word' quite clearly has proclamation to believers centrally in view, as 'suggested by the imperatives following the [*kēryxon*] charge, the inclusion of [*didachē*] in the final phrase, and the suggestion that his addressees were "turning away" from their earlier beliefs'.[37]

In addition to these instances where there are strong contextual grounds for understanding that believers were addressed by the proclamation, many other references to proclamation in the epistles cannot exclude believers as addressees.[38] In sum, the three proclamation verbs under consideration are used in a range of passages within the New Testament where the discourse context indicates that believers were (or in some cases, may have been) addressees.

3. We have noted that the 'preaching' to which our three key verbs refer in the New Testament is usually carried out by figures of recognized authority. It is possible to make a slightly more specific observation in

---

alternative proposals results in a reading of Rom. 1:15 that is natural within its context or ultimately persuasive (see Gaventa 2011: 65–75). The text should be taken at face value: Paul longs to come to Rome that he may 'preach the gospel' to the believers there (so, for instance, Cranfield 1985b: 16; Moo 1996: 62–63; Bowers 1987: 195–198). See also O'Brien 1993: 61–65, who takes the view that Rom. 1:15 refers 'to the whole range of evangelistic and teaching ministry – from the initial proclamation of the gospel to the building up of believers and grounding them firmly in the faith' (64).

[35] Smith 2012: 187.

[36] O'Brien 1993: 64; *contra* Evans 1981: 318, who suggests that 'proclamation' refers only to the initial evangelistic activity, while 'warning' and 'teaching' refer to Paul's ongoing ministry of edification. Such a separation cannot be established from the text and seems unnatural to it.

[37] Smith 2012: 171. See our more detailed treatment of this charge in the exegetical treatment of 2 Timothy in Part 2.

[38] From the literature she surveys, Smith (2012: 177) suggests the following as possibly including believers as addressees: 1 Cor. 1:23; 2:4; 9:27; 15:11, 12, 14; 1 Tim. 3:16; Titus 1:3.

light of all the data outlined above: for those who engage in 'preaching' or 'proclamation' (where the three key verbs are used), there is typically record within the New Testament of a command or commissioning of some kind for them to do so. This is the case for the angel who came to Zechariah (Luke 1:19); for John the Baptist (Matt. 3:1–3; see also Mark 1:2–7); for Jesus (Luke 4:18–19; 4:43); for the apostles (Mark 3:14; 6:7–13; [16:15]; Matt. 10:7, 27; Luke 9:2; Acts 10:42; 16:10 [here including Paul's associates]; 1 Cor. 1:17; Gal. 1:16; Eph. 3:8); and for Timothy (2 Tim. 4:2; cf. 1 Tim. 4:14; 2 Tim. 1:6).

4. Furthermore, it is significant that none of our three 'semi-technical' verbs for preaching the gospel are used anywhere in the New Testament to frame an instruction, command or commission for believers in general to 'preach'. Where there are generalized instructions in the New Testament for believers to communicate God's word, these instructions are expressed using other vocabulary.[39]

5. While the observations of this chapter confirm the suggestion that the three 'semi-technical' verbs of proclamation generally function as close equivalents in the New Testament, they also highlight some degree of distinction between them (here we will focus on the two most frequently occurring of the verbs, *euangelizomai* and *kēryssō*). In particular, the findings above suggest that although *euangelizomai* and *kēryssō* often function as close equivalents and could be used interchangeably in many instances in the New Testament,[40] nevertheless they are not exact synonyms.[41]

At this point in the discussion it is important to remember the general principle that words do not have a concrete and tightly defined single meaning, but rather are capable of conveying a range of meanings depending on the context in which they are used (this range is often referred to as a word's 'semantic range').[42] On any given occasion when a particular word is used, only part of that range of

[39] See further discussion in chapter 3.
[40] On the basis of the four Pauline epistles she analyses, and drawing particular attention to texts where the verbs in question 'are collocated and denote the same activity' (see 1 Cor. 2:1–4; 9:14–27; 15:1–14), Smith (2012: 202) concludes that they 'can function as virtual synonyms'.
[41] *Contra* Friedrich, TDNT 2.718.
[42] This very brief discussion of lexical semantics is necessarily simplified. For a more substantial introduction see Cotterell and Turner 1989: 129–187, esp. 178–181; and for guidance on further introductory literature see Klein, Blomberg and Hubbard 2004: 241, fn. 63.

meaning will be intended. For some words this range will be wider than for others, but the principle holds true for all words. It can be helpful to picture the range of meaning of a word as a circle. Nearest the centre of the circle will be meanings that are most commonly signified by the word in question.[43] Further out will be other related meanings or nuances which the word sometimes signifies, but less often. The way in which the reader determines which particular meaning is signified in any given use of the term is by considering the discourse context in which the word is being used. That is why it is always vital to take adequate account of the context of words as they appear within sentences and paragraphs (and larger units too) within any work of literature – and not least when studying books of the Bible.

The survey of the use of the verbs *euangelizomai* and *kēryssō* in this chapter indicates that they have overlapping ranges of meaning (picture the overlapping circles of a Venn diagram), but their respective ranges of meaning are not identical.

At the centre of the range of meaning of *euangelizomai* as it is used in the New Testament is the idea of making known or announcing good news (which is no surprise; the *euangelion*, or gospel, is a closely related term). That is, at the centre of the circle is a focus on the thing – good news – that is made known in the activity denoted by *euangelizomai*. Within the New Testament the 'good news' in view is the Christian gospel (the *euangelion*).[44] Most of the time, the act of communication denoted by *euangelizomai* is carried out in a public context by a person of recognized authority. Thus the normal meaning of *euangelizomai* in the New Testament is 'to preach the gospel'.

However, on a few occasions the communication referred to by *euangelizomai* is less formal and made by a variety of people (whose identity is not always specified). While our survey of New Testament occurrences of the verb confirms that the substance and character of the message are absolutely central within the range of meaning of *euangelizomai*, it also indicates that the mode and agency of the communication are less central. As we have seen, it can be used to specify the delivery of a good message by an angel to an individual

[43] These meanings will include referential, connotative, denotative and contextual meanings. See the helpful brief discussion of these types of meaning in Klein, Blomberg and Hubbard 2004: 9.

[44] The sole exception to this is the occurrence of the verb at 1 Thess. 3:6. The occurrences of *euangelizomai* in Gal. 1:8, 9 refer to the proclamation of a 'different' (i.e. false) gospel under the pretence of proclaiming the true gospel, but the sense of the verb is unchanged.

(Luke 1:19) or a group (Luke 2:10). It can refer to the public ministry of John the Baptist (Luke 3:18) and of Jesus himself (Luke 4:18, 43). It can refer to 'gospelling' carried out by apostles and others (Acts 15:35), both publicly and from house to house (Acts 5:42), and even on a one-to-one basis (Acts 8:35).

Although *euangelizomai* is indeed a 'semi-technical' term for 'announcing' the gospel, it has a wider semantic range than 'preach the gospel'. Put another way, the verb *euangelizomai* must not be identified precisely with the concept of preaching the gospel. Although the word and concept overlap quite considerably (and thus the term is rightly designated 'semi-technical'), they are not to be equated.

That is why even a translation such as the ESV, which strives to translate important Greek terms using the same English word as consistently as possible (see the ESV Preface), nonetheless translates this verb using a variety of English terms depending on the context: speakers 'bring' (Luke 1:19; 8:1; Acts 13:32; 14:15; 1 Thess. 3:6), 'tell' (Acts 8:35) and 'announce' (Rev. 10:7) good news, alongside 'preaching' and 'proclaiming' it. This is quite understandable; such a variety of English renderings accurately reflects the semantic range of the verb.

This point is important to note, because a failure to recognize (1) the breadth of the semantic range of *euangelizomai* and (2) the distinction between the verb itself and the concept of preaching the gospel (which it normally signifies in the NT) could lead us to some erroneous conclusions. In particular, failure to recognize these things might lead us to conclude that our understanding of the concept of preaching would need to incorporate the features present in *every* occurrence of *euangelizomai* in the New Testament, including the occasional uses of the term where it clearly does not mean 'to preach' and where more informal and non-public modes of communicating the gospel are signified.

When it comes to *kēryssō* the situation is somewhat different: the lexical range of the verb in the New Testament is arguably narrower, and the central focus of the semantic range is different. At the centre of the range of meaning of *kēryssō* is *the act* of authoritative public proclamation. It usually means something like 'declare aloud', 'proclaim'. The verb itself does not specify the substance of the message being proclaimed, but is normally paired with an object to give us that information ('preach *the word*'; 'he preached *the good news*'; see Matt. 4:23; 9:35; 24:14; Mark 14:9; Luke 9:2; Acts 20:25; 28:31, etc.). It is centrally a verb that points to a mode of communication (proclaiming aloud, preaching), rather than to the communication of a particular message. With very few exceptions within the New Testament, *kēryssō* is used in contexts indicating that it speaks of the public proclamation of an authoritative message by a person of recognized authority. This pattern resonates strongly with the use of the term in the Septuagint, where typically (and quite consistently) it is used to signify the public proclamation of an urgent message by a person of authority (usually someone of delegated authority: the herald of a ruler of Israel or of a foreign nation, or, frequently, a prophet of God).[45] It is no accident that the ESV, which will translate *euangelizomai* using a range of terms, restricts itself to translating *kēryssō* as 'preach' or 'proclaim' on all but one occasion.[46]

The term *kēryssō* in the New Testament is a more specialized term with a narrower range of meaning than *euangelizomai*. Although *euangelizomai* is used in places where *kēryssō* could be used (because public proclamation of the good news is in view),[47] *kēryssō* is used quite consistently in the New Testament to refer to the public proclamation of God's word (usually the gospel and its implications, broadly speaking) made by a person of authority.[48]

The observations of this chapter highlight the significance of all three of the semi-technical preaching verbs for our study, and the par-

[45] So, rightly, Mounce 1960: 14–18. See LXX Gen. 41:43; Exod. 32:5; 36:6; 2 Kgs 10:20; 2 Chr. 20:3; 24:9; 36:22; Esth. 6:9, 11; Prov. 1:21; 8:1; Isa. 61:1; Dan. 5:29; Hos. 5:8; Joel 2:1, 15; 3:9; Jon. 1:2; 3:2, 4, 5, 7; Mic. 3:5; Zeph. 3:14; Zech. 9:9.

[46] The sole exception is Mark 1:45, where, as noted above, the man healed of leprosy 'proclaims' what Jesus has done for him, in direct contravention of the instruction of Jesus (1:44).

[47] The terms thus have an overlapping range of meaning and can be used synonymously in some contexts (as already noted), but they are not absolute synonyms (*contra* Friedrich, TDNT 2.718). Bullinger's lexicon recognizes the distinction between these terms and captures at least part of the substance of that distinction in affirming that *kēryssō* 'simply regards the making known, without any reference to *the contents*, which is done by' *euangelizomai* ('Preach' in Bullinger 1908).

[48] The use of the two verbs in close proximity in Acts 8:4–5 certainly resonates with our findings here. After the martyrdom of Stephen and the scattering of believers, we read that 'those who were scattered went about preaching [*euangelizomenoi*] the word. Philip went down to the city of Samaria and proclaimed [*ekēryssen*] to them Christ.' The people mentioned in v. 4 are simply members of the church in Jerusalem (v. 1), and we know nothing of the context or manner of their 'gospelling', signified using *euangelizomai*. However, the proclamation referred to in v. 5 using the verb *kēryssō* is done by Philip, a recognized leader, and v. 6 makes it clear that the context was public: 'And the crowds with one accord paid attention to what was being said by Philip when they heard him and saw the signs that he did.'

ticular significance of *kēryssō* as the verb with the narrowest semantic range corresponding most closely and most regularly to our working definition of 'preaching'. In the exegetical studies that follow, we will pay close attention to this vocabulary as it occurs (and especially to *kēryssō*, which appears most frequently in the selected passages).

Excursus 1: The identity of the preachers in Philippians 1:14–18

The use of the term *kēryssō* at Philippians 1:15 and *katangellō* at Philippians 1:17 and 1:18 are possible exceptions to the pattern of use we have identified for those verbs in the New Testament, so this passage requires special comment. Centrally at issue here is the identity of the agents of proclamation, whom Paul identifies as 'the brothers'. Having affirmed that his imprisonment in Rome has 'served to advance the gospel' (1:12–13), Paul goes on to specify that these events have emboldened many of 'the brothers' in gospel proclamation.

> And most of the brothers [*tōn adelphōn*], having become confident in the Lord by my imprisonment, are much more bold to speak the word without fear.
>   Some indeed preach Christ from envy and rivalry, but others from good will. The latter do it out of love, knowing that I am put here for the defence of the gospel. The former proclaim Christ out of rivalry, not sincerely but thinking to afflict me in my imprisonment. What then? Only that in every way, whether in pretence or in truth, Christ is proclaimed, and in that I rejoice. (Phil. 1:14–18)

The uninterrupted flow of logic from verse 14 to the following verses indicates that the two groups of preachers Paul refers to in verses 15–18 are subsections of the larger group of 'brothers' who have been emboldened to speak in verse 14.[1] What is less clear is whether, in discussing these 'brothers', Paul is referring to the whole of the church family in Rome (implicitly, 'brothers and sisters'), or

---

[1] '[*Tines*], "some", which immediately begins v 15, is a pronoun whose antecedent most logically and naturally is taken to be [*adelphōn*], "brothers" (v 14)' (Hawthorne and Martin 2004: 45). For further support for this reading and references to those who dispute it, see O'Brien 1991: 98.

more narrowly to co-workers in proclamation.[2] This question is significant for the present study, because if Paul refers to the whole church family, these verses would stand in the New Testament as a rare (and possibly unique) attestation to believers in general, rather than leaders specifically, legitimately engaging in 'preaching'.

In favour of the view that the 'brothers' are Christians in general rather than particular co-workers are the following two significant considerations. First, the term *adelphoi* is used frequently in the New Testament to refer to Christians in general ('brothers and sisters'). Second, the term has been used with that clear meaning in the immediate context at 1:12 with reference to the Philippian Christians.

In favour of the view that here Paul refers specifically to co-workers are the following considerations.[3] First, as E. Earle Ellis pointed out some years ago, the term 'brothers' (especially when occurring in the plural with the article)[4] appears to refer specifically to ministry co-workers on quite a number of occasions in a range of New Testament books.[5] Second, Paul uses the term with this meaning elsewhere within Philippians. This is quite possibly the meaning of the term at 2:25, where Paul refers to Epaphroditus as 'my brother [*ton adelphon*] and fellow worker and fellow soldier'. It is quite clearly the case in Paul's closing greeting at 4:21–22, where Paul distinguishes between 'the brothers' and 'all the saints': 'The brothers [*hoi adelphoi*] who are with me greet you. All the saints greet you, especially those of Caesar's household.' That Paul uses the term 'brothers' at 4:21–22 to mean co-workers is widely acknowledged, including by those who would not see such a significance to the term at 1:14.[6] Third, at 2:19–30 Paul returns to the theme of 1:12–18 – that is, the encouragement and disappointment he has drawn from other believers at Rome – and there it is clear that he is referring to co-workers in particular (with

---

[2] Scholarly opinion on this question is divided, with a majority of commentators taking the view that the 'brothers' here are believers in general. For a detailed list of bibliographical references relating to this question, see Keown 2008: 75.

[3] For a compelling articulation of the case for this reading and for further lexical and exegetical detail in support of some of the points raised here, see Dickson 2003: 144–152.

[4] Note that the article is absent in Phil. 1:12, where the reference is clearly to believers in general.

[5] Ellis (1971: 445–451) suggests that this is the case in a wide range of passages, but draws particular attention to passages in Paul's letters where he appears to draw a distinction between 'the brothers' and believers in general (see 1 Cor. 16:19–20; Eph. 6:23–24; Phil. 4:21–22; Col. 4:15).

[6] So, for instance, O'Brien 1991: 553.

Timothy and Epaphroditus named), rather than the church family in general. Since his comments at 2:19–30 resonate strongly with his comments at 1:15–18, and since Paul sees little need to provide much by way of introduction to these figures at 2:19–30, it seems likely that the same group of co-workers is in view in the two passages.[7]

The factors listed above indicate quite strongly that Paul refers to particular co-workers at 1:14–15, but on their own they may not establish the position conclusively. However, if we add into the equation the findings of the previous chapter concerning the patterns of use of the verbs *katangellō* and *kēryssō* throughout the New Testament, this reading receives significant further support. As we found there, these two verbs are used with a high degree of consistency throughout the New Testament to refer to the activity of proclamation carried out by recognized and commissioned leaders. The fact that these two verbs are used to refer to the activity of proclamation in Philippians 1:15–18 adds further weight to the view that Paul is speaking here of proclamation carried out by particular co-workers and not by the whole of the church family. Holding to the reading that identifies the 'brothers' as Christians in general would require us to see here an atypical use of both verbs. Thus, in light of these lexical considerations and the contextual exegetical factors outlined above, we can conclude that Paul refers in 1:14–18 to the preaching activity of particular co-workers, rather than of believers in general. The use of the verbs *katangellō* and *kēryssō* in these verses does not, therefore, constitute an exception to the pattern of use within the New Testament outlined in the previous chapter, but rather corresponds with it.

[7] Jewett 1970: 369–371.

Chapter Three

The word ministries
of all believers

Preaching is not the only ministry of the word envisaged or mandated by Scripture. To isolate preaching from other ministries of the word or to claim that it is the sole ministry of the word is 'to make preaching carry a load which it cannot bear; that is, the burden of doing all that the Bible expects of every form of the ministry of the Word'.[1] Although the central concern of this study is to discover what the New Testament teaches about preaching as a particular ministry of the word, our survey of the language related to preaching has already raised the matter of other ministries of the word and their relationship to preaching. A comprehensive analysis of the New Testament's teaching on wider ministries of the word would be a separate and substantial study on its own, but a few brief comments and observations (particularly in light of previous scholarly discussions) are in order here.

There has been significant discussion in recent years within New Testament studies and missiological studies concerning whether the New Testament calls believers as a whole to participate in evangelistic mission.[2] We noted in the previous chapter that the New Testament nowhere calls or commands believers as a whole group to 'preach' the gospel. What are we to make of this observation? Should we conclude that, apart from leaders with a commission to preach, believers in general do not have a role to play in word-based evangelism? The answer to that question is clearly and decisively 'no'. A number of studies have demonstrated that the New Testament expects and instructs believers to engage in word-based evangelism, and reflects the reality that believers in early churches were already engaged in outreach of that kind.[3]

[handwritten margin note: Evanglism is a call for all ppl, not just pastors]

---

[1] Adam 1996: 59; quoted by Keller, who also makes the same point (Keller 2015: 5).

[2] See e.g. Dickson 2003; Ware 2005; O'Brien 1993; Plummer 2006; Liubinskas 2013; Marshall 2000; and Bowers 1991.

[3] See esp. O'Brien 1993 (as well as the brief summary of his position in Köstenberger and O'Brien 2001: 191–199); Plummer 2006; Ware 2005; and Marshall 2000. Although the position adopted on some points of exegesis in this present study would differ from a few found in these works (notably on Phil. 1:14–18; see Excursus 1), the broader position that they advocate is well established.

Paul says of the Thessalonian believers that, 'not only has the word of the Lord sounded forth from you in Macedonia and Achaia, but your faith in God has gone forth everywhere, so that we need not say anything' (1 Thess. 1:8).[4] Peter exhorts believers who face pressure and opposition to be 'prepared to make a defence to anyone who asks you for a reason for the hope that is in you' (1 Pet. 3:15). In a passage that has been named 'the Pauline Great Commission', Paul calls the believers at Ephesus to fasten on 'the belt of truth', put on 'the readiness given by the gospel of peace' and take hold of the 'sword of the Spirit, which is the word of God' (Eph. 6:13–17).[5] As O'Brien and Plummer both argue, the nature of the living word of God and the gospel message itself are such that they naturally propel and perpetuate evangelistic outreach by believers.[6]

Not only does the New Testament expect all believers to be involved in word-based evangelism, it also expects all believers to be engaged in word-based ministries of encouragement and discipleship within the church family.[7] In Colossians 3:16 Paul urges the believers in the church at Colossae to 'Let the word of Christ dwell in you richly, teaching and admonishing one another in all wisdom'. In 1 Thessalonians 5:14 Paul instructs the Thessalonian believers to serve one another in similar ways: 'And we urge you, brothers, admonish the idle, encourage the faint-hearted, help the weak, be patient with them all.' At Crete, Titus is to ensure that the older women are equipped to 'teach what is good [kalodidaskalous], and so train the young women to love their husbands and children, to be self-controlled, pure, working at home, kind and submissive to their own husbands, that the word of God may not be reviled' (Titus 2:3–5). Older women are to teach younger women principles from the word of God so that the younger women will live out those principles and not cause the word to be reviled. The writer of Hebrews calls the believers to 'exhort [or 'encourage', parakaleite] one another every day, as long as it is called "today", that none of you may be hardened by the deceitfulness of sin' (Heb. 3:13; similarly 10:25). Hebrews can describe the words of Scripture themselves as 'encouragement'/'exhortation' (paraklēsis) at 12:5, and the immediate context here in chapter 3 indicates that 'today' is the day when God's voice is

[margin handwritten note: All believers called to discipleship]

---

[4] On the spread of the gospel through the Thessalonian believers, see further Ware 1992.

[5] O'Brien 1993: 109–131.

[6] O'Brien 1993: passim; Plummer 2006: passim; see also Ware 1992: 128–130.

[7] For a recent and detailed consideration of the wide-ranging involvement of all believers in the teaching of God's word in the Pauline churches, see Smith 2012.

heard (see 3:7). This suggests that the activity of 'encouragement' the believers are to engage in shares something of the character of God's word, presumably because the activity will consist of calling others to respond appropriately to the voice of God as it is heard in Scripture (probably here, in the *preaching of Scripture*).[8]

In these examples, believers in general are called to 'teach', 'admonish' and 'encourage' one another with the word of God. These and other texts demonstrate the expectation that all believers should exercise word ministry within the fellowship. It is significant to note that none of these examples cited constitutes an injunction for all believers to 'preach'. However, further observation of these texts yields evidence suggesting both an overlap with and an interplay between the word ministry of believers in general and that of church leaders in particular. In Colossians 3:16 Paul instructs the believers to 'Let the word of Christ dwell in you richly, teaching [*didaskontes*] and admonishing [*nouthetountes*] one another in all wisdom'. Strikingly, earlier in the same letter Paul has used just the same language to refer to his own preaching ministry: 'Him we proclaim [*katangellomen*], warning [or 'admonishing', *nouthetountes*] everyone and teaching [*didaskontes*] everyone with all wisdom' (Col. 1:28). Clearly their ministry to each other takes its cue from the ministry of the apostle Paul, and parallels his in significant ways.

The charge to the Thessalonian believers to minister to one another in 1 Thessalonians 5 follows the charge to respond rightly to those in leadership who minister to them. What is of interest here is that Paul uses the same verb in verse 12 to speak of the ministry of the leaders that he will use in verse 14 to speak of the ministry of the believers to each other:

We ask you, brothers, to respect those who labour among you and are over you in the Lord and admonish [*nouthetountas*] you,[9] and to esteem them very highly in love because of their work. Be at peace among yourselves. And we urge you, brothers, admonish [*noutheteite*] the idle.' (1 Thess. 5:12–4)

Again, the ministry of the whole church family to one another is to parallel the ministry of its leaders. It seems reasonable to suggest that the admonishments the believers within the fellowship give each other

---

[8] See further discussion of this point below.
[9] Note that this is the same verb again that Paul used at Col. 3:16 with reference to his preaching.

should flow from the admonishments they have received from their leaders. These need not come exclusively through the public preaching of the leaders, but it would surely include this. More than that, it seems natural that the admonishments of believers to one another would carry more weight if they plainly reinforced what had been publicly taught from Scripture by the leaders.

The instructions for the older women at Crete to 'teach what is good' [kalodidaskalous] to the younger women (Titus 2:3–5) fall within a section where Paul is telling Titus what he should teach in the church at Crete: 'But as for you, teach [lit. 'speak'] what accords with sound doctrine [didaskalia]' (2:1). Paul does not explicitly identify this teaching of Titus as 'preaching', but his instructions concerning the manner in which Titus is to teach suggest that he has in mind an authoritative public declaration: 'Declare these things; exhort and rebuke with all authority. Let no one disregard you' (2:15). In his public ministry, Titus is to speak in accordance with 'sound teaching' so that the older women will be equipped to 'teach what is good'. The word ministry of the older women is to flow directly from the public ministry of Titus. Presumably its central content will derive from the ministry of Titus, and it will act to reinforce that public word ministry.

The writer of Hebrews' call for the believers to 'exhort [or 'encourage', parakaleite] one another' (3:13; 10:25) mirrors his own concern and activity in the discourse. Hebrews is characterized by frequent exhortations to respond to God's word, and the writer identifies his discourse as a 'word of exhortation' (logos tēs paraklēseōs, 13:22). As we will argue later in our more detailed treatment of Hebrews, the letter is itself probably written as a sermon, designed to be read out to the congregation. The writer's sermon is an 'encouragement'/'exhortation' (drawing upon the 'encouragement'/'exhortation' of Scripture; see 12:5), which in turn calls the addressees to 'exhort'/'encourage' one another. In chapter 3 the 'exhortation' that the believers are to issue to one another flows from the experience of hearing God's voice 'today' (3:7, 13). This experience can hardly exclude (and may primarily constitute) the hearing of God's voice through the Hebrews sermon as it is preached to them 'today'.[10] It is no coincidence that the second call for believers to 'exhort' one another (10:25) comes at the end of the longest section of exhortations in the discourse (10:19–25); the

---

[10] For a further exploration of these and related matters, see our more detailed treatment of Hebrews in chapter 9.

exhortations of the believers to one another are presumably to be shaped by the exhortations of the Hebrews sermon. Once again, in the case of Hebrews, the ministry of believers to one another flows from and reinforces the preaching ministry they receive.

Nowhere does the New Testament call or instruct believers as a whole group to 'preach', but it does call them to minister the word to one another, and does so using language that can also describe preaching. The instructions for believers to engage in word ministry that we have seen above are framed without using the three 'semi-technical' preaching verbs identified in chapter 2. This fact supports the contention that preaching has a distinct character as a particular ministry of the word. At the same time, the fact that the vocabulary used to frame these more generalized instructions is also applied to preaching in various contexts in the New Testament tends to affirm the close affinity and integral interrelationship between preaching and other ministries of the word.

We are called to minister to all others through God's Word

Part II:
Exegetical studies

Chapter Four

2 Timothy 3 – 4:
The preacher's charge

The charge of 2 Timothy 4:2 to 'preach the word' is the centrepiece of this section of the discourse and arguably constitutes the climax of 2 Timothy as a whole. The fact that this charge is given 'in the presence of God and of Christ Jesus' and in light of his return as judge and king (4:1) highlights its solemnity and significance. The charge is noteworthy within the New Testament because few other passages give explicit instructions about preaching. Moreover, it is arguably the New Testament passage concerning preaching that most clearly and directly applies to pastor-teachers in the post-apostolic age.[1] An analysis of the charge of 4:2 within its discourse context yields a number of observations that are significant for our analysis of the New Testament's portrayal of preaching and that resonate with what we have found so far. Four merit particular attention here.

Paul's charge to Timothy establishes a bridge between apostolic and post-apostolic preaching

There is much biblical material that speaks of the preaching of others (OT prophets, Jesus, the apostles), but very rarely does the New Testament speak explicitly of the preaching of post-apostolic church leaders. Here in 2 Timothy 4, Timothy is the person addressed. Timothy is sometimes termed an 'apostolic agent' by commentators and theologians; he was directly chosen, trained, appointed and dispatched by Paul. The same will not be true, of course, for modern preachers. However, Paul writes to Timothy at the end of his own life and ministry (2 Tim. 4:6) with a clear awareness that the baton of ministry is passing on from him (the apostle) to Timothy and to those who will follow. Seen in that light, Timothy acts as a vital bridge for

---

[1] Hence the decision to begin the exegetical studies with this key passage. Subsequent studies are presented in canonical order.

us when it comes to our understanding of the Bible's pattern for pastoral ministry in general and preaching ministry in particular.

Reflecting on his own ministry, Paul writes in the first chapter of 2 Timothy that he was 'appointed a preacher [*kēryx*] and apostle and teacher' of the gospel (1:11). Paul's apostleship is grounded in his personal encounter with Jesus and his commission from Jesus. Obviously, that aspect of his ministry is not transferable. However, Paul indicates that the roles of 'preacher' and 'teacher' are transferable, and should be perpetuated beyond his ministry. Paul is conscious that, as a preacher, apostle and teacher, he has been entrusted with the stewardship of the gospel in a special way. Although that stewardship has led to suffering and to imprisonment (2 Tim. 1:8, 16; a fact that could make him something of a pessimist for the future), Paul knows that God is more than able to guard the gospel for the future: 'I know whom I have believed, and I am convinced that he is able to guard until that Day what has been entrusted to me' (2 Tim. 1:12).[2] 'That Day' is the Day of Jesus' return (see 4:8). So Paul believes that the stewardship of the gospel – a stewardship which in his ministry has been expressed through his preaching and teaching – will continue for the whole of the church's age, until Jesus returns.

In the next breath he calls upon Timothy to follow in his footsteps: 'Follow the pattern of the sound words that you have heard from me, in the faith and love that are in Christ Jesus. By the Holy Spirit who dwells within us, guard the good deposit entrusted to you' (2 Tim. 1:13–14). Timothy is to pick up the baton of gospel stewardship from Paul. Presumably this will involve, not apostleship, but preaching and teaching. After all, the idea of stewarding an urgent, life-giving message (see 1:8–10) cannot mean simply locking it away safely. It must mean communicating it.

Paul returns to this charge but extends its scope at the beginning of chapter 2: 'You then, my child, be strengthened by the grace that is in Christ Jesus, and what you have heard from me in the presence of many witnesses entrust to faithful men who will be able to teach others also' (2 Tim. 2:1–2). Now Paul has in view not only Timothy's ministry, but the ministry of the generations who will follow him.

---

[2] The alternative reading of v. 12, that Paul is convinced that God is able to guard what he (Paul) has entrusted to him, is less likely on the grounds, first, that v. 14 speaks of the apostolic gospel as a deposit 'entrusted' to Timothy (see also 1 Tim. 6:20), and, second, that it would seem uncharacteristic for Paul to emphasize the kind of self-concern that would be implied by this reading. Note also that the preferred reading coheres better with the instruction of 2:2. (Kelly 1963: 165–166.)

Timothy is to pass on the gospel message and its stewardship (and therefore its preaching and teaching) to 'faithful men' of a coming generation, who will themselves 'be able to teach others also'. Gospel stewardship through preaching and teaching will continue beyond Timothy. And, crucially, what Timothy learns from Paul about that stewardship (especially through this present letter, 2 Timothy) he is to pass on to the next generation of preachers and teachers.

The same dynamic is found in the context of the key charge of 4:2. Paul issues the solemn charge to Timothy to 'preach the word' and, after discussing what will be involved in doing so, gives a reason why it is so important that Timothy should heed it: 'For I am already being poured out as a drink offering, and the time of my departure has come' (4:6). Timothy must preach the word because Paul's preaching days are drawing to a close.[3]

Paul thus establishes a traceable line of continuity from his apostolic preaching ministry to the preaching ministry of apostolic agents like Timothy, and then to the preaching ministry of those who follow. The baton of preaching (but not of apostolicity or associated miracle-working[4]) is passed on from one generation to the next. All that leads us to the conclusion that the charge to 'preach the word' applies not only to Timothy, but to all those who will follow as pastor-teachers down through the ages, until the return of Christ.

Timothy is to make an authoritative proclamation of God's word

The charge that Paul gives Timothy is not simply 'to preach', but to 'preach *the word*' (2 Tim. 4:2). The context makes it clear that 'the word' here is Scripture – and particularly its message of 'salvation through faith in Christ Jesus' (3:15). At the end of chapter 3 Paul impressed upon Timothy the sufficiency of Scripture for his ministry (3:16–17) so that, unlike the false teachers mentioned earlier in the letter, Timothy will stick with Scripture as the all-sufficient basis of

---

[3] A similar pattern is reflected in Titus. Paul is established as a preacher with a stewardship (1:2–3). Titus is left in Crete to appoint elders as stewards of God's work (1:5, 7), who will hold firm to the word he has received and teach it with authority (1:9). Titus himself must also minister the word that he has received from Paul with a God-given authority: 'Declare these things; exhort and rebuke with all authority. Let no one disregard you' (2:15).

[4] These belonged to that crucial first generation of proclamation and served to authenticate the gospel as proclaimed by Jesus and the apostles. See Acts 2:22; Heb. 2:1–4; 2 Cor. 12:2.

his ministry, for the long run. Then follows the charge of 4:1–2, which spells out the precise way in which Timothy is to use this sufficient Scripture.

The charge is made up of five verbs in the imperative ('preach the word', 'be ready in season and out of season', 'reprove', 'rebuke' and 'exhort') followed by a prepositional phrase that qualifies them ('with complete patience and teaching'). Although each of the five imperatives carries its own weight and meaning and could seem like one of a series of stand-alone instructions, the leading charge to 'preach the word' 'plays a dominant role, not only by being first but also by being amplified by the second imperative "be ready in season and out of season", and by the prepositional phrase with [didachē] at the end of this verse'.[5] If the five imperatives were really stand-alone instructions (rather than the four relating closely to the first), the second charge would carry little meaning; the charge 'be ready' as a stand-alone charge immediately begs the question: Be ready to do what?

If the leading imperative 'preach' (kēryxon) is qualified by the four imperatives and the prepositional phrase that follow, each of these then communicates something of the nature of the preaching that Timothy is to engage in. To obey the charge to preach will require Timothy to be ready (epistēthi) 'in season and out of season',[6] not least because sound teaching will not always be welcome (4:3). In his preaching, Timothy will have to 'reprove' (elenxon; that is, correct false understanding or sinful behaviour), 'rebuke' (epitimēson; that is, call his addressees to turn from ungodliness) and 'exhort' (parakaleson; that is, call the people to believe and live out the truth he proclaims). He is to do all this with 'patience' (makrothymia), because it will take time and perseverance for his addressees to accept and respond to God's word. And he is to preach with 'teaching' (didachē), because his reprovals, rebukes and exhortations will only carry weight and be effective if they are grounded in a clear articulation and explanation of what the word of God says. Preaching the word cannot be reduced to teaching it (in the sense of simply explaining the meaning of the word as a purely didactic activity); it involves the urgent call to respond that is signified by the imperatives 'reprove, rebuke and exhort'. At the same time, preaching for Timothy will always fundamentally involve teaching and can never happen apart from teaching.

The character of preaching as presented here in 4:2 is of an

---

[5] Knight 1992: 453.
[6] This could refer either to Timothy's own 'season' of readiness to preach, or that of his addressees to hear. Quite possibly both are in view.

'authoritative and educational' proclamation of God's word.[7] Timothy will patiently teach the meaning of God's word and urge people to make an appropriate response to it.

Timothy's preaching is to address the believers in Ephesus (to believers)

It is sometimes noted that most of the instances where the verb *kēryssō* is used in the New Testament point to a proclamation of the gospel to unbelievers.[8] As already noted, that should come as no great surprise; the Gospels and Acts are largely (but not exclusively) taken up with first-contact evangelism, and much of the 'preaching' that we observe in the New Testament is in those books. However, it would be a false step to assume on the basis of that observation that 'preaching' is primarily or exclusively an evangelistic activity directed towards unbelievers.[9] The framing of the charge here in 2 Timothy 4:2 tells against such a conclusion.

The scriptural 'word' that is to be the substance of Timothy's proclamation equips him 'for teaching, for reproof, for correction, and for training in righteousness' (3:16), and so, in his preaching, he is to 'reprove, rebuke, and exhort, with complete patience and teaching' (4:2). These are functions that we would naturally associate, not with first-contact evangelism, but rather with the edification of God's people; and that is evidently the context that Paul has in mind. He is concerned about the danger of believers turning to false teaching (4:3–4; see 2:16–18; 3:1–9), and Timothy's proclamation of the word will be a necessary safeguard for the believers in that place.[10] Paul warns that 'the time is coming' when those who currently sit under

---

[7] Smith 2012: 171.

[8] Evans 1981: 316.

[9] This is the surprising conclusion that Evans (1981) reaches, going so far as to suggest that preaching a monologue to a congregation of believers can be 'detrimental' (321–322). He recognizes that 2 Tim. 4:2 is an exception to the NT pattern he finds, but he maintains that the aorist tense of *kēryxon* indicates that the activity is to be occasional (the declaration of the gospel as a specific response to heresy) rather than a regular part of the life of the church (318). To draw such a conclusion on the basis of the use of the aorist tense here is quite unjustified. As Wallace rightly notes, in the case of an aorist imperative 'the force generally is to *command the action as a whole*, without focusing on duration, repetition, etc. . . . the aorist puts forth a *summary command*' (Wallace 1996: 485; italics his). The aorist used here is a constative aorist (so Wallace 1996: 721 and Mounce 2000: 573), serving to highlight the solemn nature of the charge and to give it the force, 'Make this your top priority' (Wallace 1996: 720–721).

[10] So Smith 2012: 171.

the word 'will not endure sound teaching' (4:3). Nonetheless, for as long as the people will listen, Timothy is to continue preaching the word to them.

The preaching ministry that Paul commissions Timothy to undertake here is primarily an ongoing ministry to the people of God. Undoubtedly that ministry will include evangelism (as is probably indicated by the instruction 'do the work of an evangelist', 4:5),[11] but the main context for Timothy's proclamation as mandated by this charge is the church in Ephesus.

Timothy is a commissioned and authoritative speaker of God's word

We have already noted the authoritative character of the proclamation Timothy is charged to make here in 4:2. A number of further features of the passage suggest that the commission Paul gives Timothy in 4:2 is a specific commission to proclaim the word *as God's authoritative representative*. The designation of Timothy as a 'man of God' (3:17) in conjunction with the charge to 'preach' (4:2) strongly suggests that Timothy's preaching ministry stands in a line of continuity with commissioned 'prophetic' word ministry throughout Scripture.

Before charging Timothy to 'preach the word' at 4:2, Paul sets out in 3:16–17 to remind him of the power and sufficiency of God's word for his ministry in Ephesus: 'All Scripture is breathed out by God and profitable for teaching, for reproof, for correction, and for training in righteousness, that the man of God may be competent, equipped for every good work.' Who, then, is this 'man of God' who is so well equipped by Scripture for every good work? Given that in the immediately following verses Paul is going to issue to Timothy a direct charge to preach those Scriptures, it is quite clear that Paul regards Timothy as such a 'man of God'.

It could be that the term 'man of God' in this context simply means 'person belonging to God': that is, any Christian person. However, the term has a substantial Old Testament pedigree as a name used to refer to God's appointed leaders of his people and, in particular, those who are sent as authoritative speakers of his word.[12] So, for instance, it is used to identify Moses (Deut. 33:1), David (2 Chr. 8:14), Samuel

---

[11] So Marshall 2000: 261; Smith 2012: 171; although see Carson 2014: 2–3.
[12] On the OT background and use of the term, see TDOT 1.233–235 and Holstein 1977.

(1 Sam. 9:6, 10), Elijah (1 Kgs 17:18, 24), Elisha (2 Kgs 4:7, 9) and an angelic messenger (Judg. 13:6–8). It can serve as a functional equivalent of the term 'prophet' (see esp. 1 Sam. 9:6, 9 and 1 Kgs 17:18, 24 with 19:16).[13] A hallmark of the man of God is that he speaks true words from God. This significance is attached to the phrase in 1 Samuel 9:6, when Saul's servant tells him about Samuel: 'Behold, there is a man of God in this city, and he is a man who is held in high honour; all that he says comes true. So now let us go there. Perhaps he can tell us the way we should go.' The same is true in 1 Kings 17, when the Lord through Elijah raises to life the son of the widow of Zarephath. The woman has already addressed Elijah as 'man of God' in verse 18, but when her son dies and is raised to life again, she says to Elijah, 'Now I know that you are a man of God, and that the word of the Lord in your mouth is truth' (1 Kgs 17:24). In other words, she is now fully assured that Elijah is a true spokesman of God because God has verified his ministry and identity as a 'man of God' through a miracle.

In 1 Timothy 6:11, Paul calls Timothy 'man of God' in a context where he has charged him to 'teach and urge' (6:2b) the things that Paul has been writing to him and where he has called Timothy to live a life that stands out in contrast to that of the false teachers. The false teachers propound a different doctrine, thinking that it will lead to gain (6:2b–5). Timothy, though, is to be different; so Paul marks the contrast (as he does a number of times in the Pastoral Epistles) using the phrase 'but you' (Gk *sy de*): 'But as for you, O man of God, flee these things. Pursue righteousness, godliness, faith, love, steadfastness, gentleness' (6:11). Timothy is to stand out as a true teacher of God's word. His life is to validate and commend his ministry as that of any authentic 'man of God'. The phrase 'man of God' here in 1 Timothy 6 is meant to indicate that 'Timothy is a man of God akin to the prophets of old'.[14]

In 2 Timothy 3:17, the broader context is likewise that of a contrast in life and doctrine between Timothy and the false teachers (see 3:6–9) that serves to validate Timothy as a true 'man of God'. As in 1 Timothy 6, Timothy is to stand out as a model of godliness and authenticity, following in Paul's footsteps: 'You, however, have followed my teaching, my conduct, my aim in life . . .' (3:10). Timothy (with all

---

[13] TDOT 1.235. Although note Holstein's (1977: 71–75) case that the two terms are not direct equivalents, but 'man of God' functions as an honorific term frequently applied to the prophets because they were typically held in high honour.

[14] Mounce 2000: 353.

believers) should be prepared for persecution, 'while evil people and impostors will go on from bad to worse, deceiving and being deceived' (3:13). Again, Timothy is to stand out in contrast to these ungodly deceivers in his adherence to the apostolic gospel and to the Scriptures: 'But as for you . . .' (3:14). Then follows the solemn charge to Timothy, the authentic 'man of God', to preach [*kēryxon*][15] the authoritative word of God (4:2).

There is a range of evidence in Paul's letters to suggest that he viewed his own ministry as standing in a line of continuity with Old Testament prophets.[16] The use of the title 'man of God' indicates that Timothy's preaching ministry will likewise stand in a line of continuity with the ministries of God's authoritative speakers throughout history, stretching back through the apostles, Jesus himself, and ultimately to the ministry of the Old Testament prophets.

Summary

In this paradigmatic charge to Timothy, and preachers who follow him, Paul calls Timothy to proclaim God's word authoritatively and didactically. The framing of the charge to preach in 2 Timothy 4:2 indicates that Timothy's preaching ministry is to address primarily (but not exclusively) the believers in the church at Ephesus. In calling Timothy to this task and identifying him as a 'man of God', Paul sets Timothy the preacher in a line of continuity with himself and his own apostolic preaching. Furthermore, he sets Timothy and preachers who follow him in a line of continuity with authoritative speakers of God's word in the Old Testament.

[15] Note that in the LXX the verb *kēryssō* was used on a number of occasions to designate prophetic declarations made by those commissioned by God (see Isa. 61:1; Joel 2:1; 3:9; Jon. 1:2; 3:2, 4; Mic. 3:5 [here, of misleading prophecy]).
[16] See Excursus 2 for further discussion.

Excursus 2:
Biblical-theological connections between New Testament preaching and Old Testament prophecy

One of the interests of this study is to set the New Testament's presentation of preaching within its broader biblical-theological framework. In the previous chapter we noted Paul's affirmation that Scripture equips 'the man of God' for every good work, including (indeed, *especially*) the work of preaching (2 Tim. 3:16 – 4:2). In light of the fact that the term 'man of God' often referred to the prophet of God in the Old Testament, these verses highlight one potentially rich vein of biblical-theological connection, namely, that the Christian preacher stands in a line of continuity with the Old Testament prophet. Is it indeed right to identify in 2 Timothy 3 – 4 an intended connection between the Christian preacher and the Old Testament prophet? Does such a connection cohere with the presentation of preaching found elsewhere in the New Testament? To answer these questions will require us to stand back from 2 Timothy and take a broader look at some evidence from the wider New Testament canon.

The first preacher we encounter in the New Testament is John the Baptist, whom the Gospels present as a figure cast in a prophetic mould. Luke's record of the angel foretelling John's birth to Zechariah makes very clear connections with Old Testament prophetic traditions:

> . . . for he will be great before the Lord . . . And he will turn many of the children of Israel to the Lord their God, and he will go before him in the spirit and power of Elijah, to turn the hearts of the fathers to the children, and the disobedient to the wisdom of the just, to make ready for the Lord a people prepared. (Luke 1:15–17)

Like Jeremiah (Jer. 1:5), John would be set apart even from the womb. Like Samuel (1 Sam. 1:11), he would be consecrated to the Lord. Just as the Old Testament prophets were occasionally given the Spirit to enable them to prophesy (1 Sam. 10:10; 2 Kgs 2:9–16; Ezek. 11:5), so he would be filled with the Spirit. He would go before the Lord 'in the spirit and power of Elijah' and do the characteristic prophetic work of calling people to repent, turn to the Lord and prepare for his coming.[1] In short, Luke's account makes it clear that 'John will be a prophet . . . he will be like Elijah in his ministry'.[2] Matthew's introduction to John the Baptist similarly presents him as a prophetic preacher with particular parallels to Elijah.[3] His ministry is further linked to the prophetic tradition of the Old Testament in that it is explicitly foretold by Isaiah:

> In those days John the Baptist came preaching in the wilderness of Judea, 'Repent, for the kingdom of heaven is at hand.' For this is he who was spoken of by the prophet Isaiah when he said,
>
> > 'The voice of one crying in the wilderness:
> > Prepare the way of the Lord;
> > make his paths straight.'
>
> Now John wore a garment of camel's hair and a leather belt round his waist, and his food was locusts and wild honey. (Matt. 3:1–4; see Mark 1:2–8)

Like Elijah (1 Kgs 17:3–7; 19:3–8, 13, 19; 2 Kgs 1:8; 2:8–14; cf. Zech. 13:4), John the Baptist spent time in the wilderness and was known for his hair garment and leather belt. No doubt these features of John's life, alongside his bold preaching ministry, fuelled the public perception that he was indeed a prophet (Matt. 21:26). Matthew makes it clear that John fulfilled the role of Elijah in his day through the announcement of the Lord's coming (see Matt. 11:9–14; 17:11–13; Mark 9:11–13; but cf. John 1:21).

The Gospels undoubtedly present John's ministry as the precursor to the ministry of Jesus. Not only do John and Jesus preach

---

[1] The description of the promised effect of John's ministry in Luke 1:17 clearly recalls the promised role of the coming Elijah in Mal. 4:5–6: 'Behold, I will send you Elijah the prophet before the great and awesome day of the LORD comes. And he will turn the hearts of fathers to their children and the hearts of children to their fathers.'
[2] Bock 1994: 36–37.
[3] France 2007: 97–107.

complementary (and significantly parallel) messages, but '[t]heir careers run parallel in significant ways: both are properly regarded as prophets, opposed by Jerusalem authorities, eventually rejected and executed, but given burial by their disciples'.[4] Wright is probably correct in his assessment that 'Jesus continued to regard him [John] as the advance guard for his own work, both as the chronological and theological starting-point for his own ministry, and as in some sense the role model for his own style, the pattern with which he would begin'.[5]

At the opening of his ministry Jesus claims for himself the role of the prophet who 'proclaims' the good news of Isaiah 61 (Luke 4:18–19) and he proceeds to devote himself to that proclamatory ministry (Luke 4:44; 8:1). Like the Gospels' portrayal of John the Baptist, the portrayal of Jesus' ministry in the Gospels at points recalls very strongly Old Testament prophetic ministries (especially the ministry of Elijah; cf. Luke 7:11–17 and 1 Kgs 17:17–24). Not only does Jesus accept and affirm the designation 'prophet' for himself (Matt. 13:57/ Mark 6:4; Luke 4:24–27; 13:33; see also Matt. 10:40–41), but a range of others, including unnamed crowds, followers and apostles, identify him as a prophet (Mark 6:14–16/Luke 9:7–9; Luke 7:16; Mark 8:28/ Matt. 16:14/Luke 9:19; Matt. 21:11, 46; John 4:19; 7:52; 9:17; see also Luke 7:39–50; Mark 14:65/Matt. 26:68/Luke 22:64; 24:19; Acts 3:22–26).[6]

While a range of material within the Gospels portrays Jesus as standing within the Old Testament prophetic traditions, elsewhere the New Testament makes it clear that he is not merely another prophet in the line of prophets.[7] He is distinct as a deliverer of God's word

[4] France 2007: 98.
[5] Wright 1996: 161–162.
[6] This summary of the evidence is drawn substantially from Wright 1996: 164–165. See further comments on some key passages there, and 165–197 for a treatment of further indications in the Gospels that Jesus is rightly seen as a prophet. The evidence of the Gospels makes it 'clear that Jesus regarded his ministry as in continuity with, and bringing to a climax, the work of the great prophets of the Old Testament, culminating in John the Baptist, whose initiative he had used as his launching-pad' (167). On the presentation of Jesus as a prophet in Luke–Acts, see further Croatto 2005. Croatto rightly highlights the sustained presentation of Jesus as prophet in Luke–Acts but is not convincing in his claim that until the cross, resurrection and ascension the presentation of Jesus as prophet dominates in favour of the presentation of Jesus as Messiah.
[7] As Wright (1996: 197) points out, if Jesus said of John the Baptist that he was 'more than a prophet' (Matt. 11:9/Luke 7:26), then 'what must be said of Jesus himself?' The category of 'prophet' is, of course, too narrow on its own to fully define his identity and work.

and bears a unique authority. Nowhere is this point established more clearly than in Hebrews 1:1–3:

> Long ago, at many times and in many ways, God spoke to our fathers by the prophets, but in these last days he has spoken to us by his Son, whom he appointed the heir of all things, through whom also he created the world. He is the radiance of the glory of God and the exact imprint of his nature.

Jesus is rightly regarded as the fulfilment of the whole trajectory of the prophetic traditions of the Old Testament. God's revelatory speech in and through him in the final era of history is complete because Jesus himself is the personal expression of God's own being. Jesus is the promised prophet like Moses – indeed, as the Son, one far greater than Moses – who brings the Old Testament prophetic office to ultimate expression and fulfilment and to whom the people of God must listen (Deut. 18:15; cf. Acts 3:22–26).[8]

The prophetic office and traditions of the Old Testament reach ultimate fulfilment in the Lord Jesus himself. However, having been fulfilled in him, they find continued expression in the new community he forms. As Jesus sends out his disciples to preach God's word just as he preached it, he signals that the work of speaking God's word is not limited to him alone. The disciples will act as agents of Jesus the great Prophet, speaking his words on his behalf. On a number of occasions Jesus indicates quite clearly that his disciples are rightly regarded as prophets, even though he does not explicitly and directly name them as such.[9] His instructions to the disciples not to make material preparations for their mission recall the Lord's instructions to Elijah (cf. Luke 9:1–6 and 1 Kgs 17:1–16), reinforcing their association with Old Testament prophets.

After the ascension the Holy Spirit is given to believers in fulfilment of the promise of Joel 2:28 that 'in the last days . . . I will pour out my Spirit on all flesh, and your sons and your daughters shall prophesy' (cited in Acts 2:17). Within its context in Acts 2, Peter's sermon at Pentecost clearly constitutes one important expression (but clearly not the only expression) of this Spirit-enabled 'prophecy', as do, arguably, the other sermons in Acts.[10] At a number of points in Acts,

---

[8] For further consideration of the links between Jesus, John the Baptist and the prophetic traditions of Israel in light of relevant scholarship, see Aernie 2012: 61–71.

[9] See Matt. 5:11–12; 10:41; 23:34; and comments in France 2007: 413.

[10] Peterson 2011.

Paul's apostolic call and ministry is related to the call and ministry of
. Old Testament prophets.[11] Furthermore, the narrative portrayal in
Acts of his trials and suffering as the means by which the gospel is
disseminated aligns Paul closely with the Servant of Isaiah.[12]

Although Paul never designates himself a 'prophet',[13] there is a range
of evidence within his letters that he views his own ministry as standing
in a line of continuity with that of the Old Testament prophets.[14] His
reference to his calling to be a preacher in Galatians 1:15–16 echoes
passages that speak of the calling of the Servant of Isaiah (Isa. 49:1–6)
and Jeremiah (Jer. 1:5).[15] Here and at a number of other points Paul
echoes or refers to passages from Isaiah's Servant Songs in the context
of a discussion of his calling and ministry, indicating (in line with the
portrayal of Paul in Acts) that 'his ministry is modelled on and a
continuance of that of the Servant'.[16] As we will see below in our
treatment of 2 Corinthians, Paul quite explicitly compares and
contrasts his ministry and that of his associates with the ministry of
Moses at points in that letter.[17] Given that Old Testament prophetic
traditions demonstrably shape Paul's self-understanding as an apostle
and preacher, his designation of Timothy the preacher as a 'man of
God' in 2 Timothy 3:17 signals that Timothy's identity and work as a
preacher are similarly shaped by those traditions.

[11] Peterson 2009: 514, esp. fn. 36.
[12] Ciampa and Rosner (2010: 12) rightly highlight this motif in Acts, although
overstate the extent to which Acts identifies Paul personally with the Servant: 'Acts
paints Paul as the Lord's Isaianic Servant, who, through suffering, trials, and rejection
by his own people, testifies to the name of the Lord and his Christ before "kings"
(Isa. 49:7). Paul in his own person takes on the prophetic role of Israel – he is the light
to the nations, the bringer of salvation.'
[13] Samra (2006: 47) notes this point and rightly suggests that it indicates that the
prophetic tradition is 'important' for Paul's apostolic self-understanding, but 'not broad
enough' to encompass all that is involved in his apostleship.
[14] For detailed analysis of this connection, and for bibliographical references to
further discussion, see Sandnes 1991 and, more recently, Aernie 2012.
[15] Ciampa 1998: 111–116; Sandnes 1991: 61–65; Schreiner 2010: 101; Bruce 1982a:
92; O'Brien 1993: 5–6; and Aernie 2012: 136–137.
[16] O'Brien (1993: 7; cf. 11–12, 20, 46) notes the following passages in this connection:
Gal. 1:15 and Isa. 49:1, 5; Rom. 15:21 and Isa. 52:15; 2 Cor. 6:2 and Isa. 49:8; Rom.
10:16 and Isa 53:1; also Acts 13:47 and Isa. 49:6; Acts 18:9, 10 and Isa. 43:5. In a
number of these passages where Paul alludes to the call and work of the Servant in
connection with his own ministry, it is clear that Paul is speaking particularly of his
preaching ministry (see Gal. 1:16; Rom. 15:20; and with wider reference to Christian
preachers in general, Rom. 10:14–15). For further works treating Paul's connection to
Isaiah's Servant see Aernie 2012: 134–135, fn. 81. We will return to the question of
Paul's self-understanding in connection with OT prophets and pursue it further in the
exegetical studies below.
[17] On that comparison, see esp. Hafemann 2005.

Taken together, these observations indicate, on one level, that New Testament preachers are not exact equivalents to Old Testament prophets. The New Testament is strikingly consistent in not naming preachers after Jesus as 'prophets' nor their proclamation as 'prophecy'. At the same time, the variety and richness of intertextual quotations, allusions and resonances that associate the preaching ministry of Jesus, the apostles (Paul in particular) and other Christian preachers in the New Testament with Old Testament prophetic traditions suggests the importance of these traditions for understanding the nature of Christian preaching. As a biblical-theological category, 'prophecy' is not sufficient to provide a complete framework for understanding what Christian preaching is, but it is unquestionably a central part of the New Testament's presentation of preaching. In sum, there is a biblical-theological line of continuity that runs from Old Testament prophets, finds fulfilment in Christ (the promised great Prophet like Moses) and then extends out from him to the church – and especially to the apostles, their agents and successors whose work it is to preach God's word.

The exegetical studies that follow (particularly of Romans and 1 and 2 Corinthians) will continue to evaluate and test this proposal.

Chapter Five

Romans 10: The preacher's commission

In Romans 9–11 Paul is addressing the difficult question of why ethnic Israel as a whole has not responded to the gospel. Within the context of addressing this question, in chapter 10 he considers the nature of the gospel and the means by which it is disseminated. A central affirmation of Romans 10 is that God makes his salvation available through the preaching of his word. Paul's initial concern is to demonstrate that God has already made full provision for the preaching of the gospel to ethnic Israel through his own ministry (and presumably that of the other apostles), so that there can be no question that God has not rejected his people (11:1). In demonstrating the mechanism by which ethnic Israel has heard the gospel in the apostolic age, however, Paul outlines the only mechanism by which anyone will hear and receive the gospel in any age.[1] Four particular observations from Romans 10 concerning the nature of preaching are important for our consideration.

Preaching reflects the nature of the gospel as something given and received

Paul begins by lamenting the fact that his own people have sought to establish their own salvation, rather than accept the salvation that God has offered them freely: 'For, being ignorant of the righteousness of God [made available through the gospel], and seeking to establish their own, they did not submit to God's righteousness' (10:3). He notes that the righteousness based on the law is founded upon doing the commandments (10:5); but the righteousness of Christ offered

---

[1] 'Probably . . . Paul writes generally in vv. 14–18 about the relationship of all people to the message of the gospel while at the same time thinking especially of the application of these points to Israel' (Moo 1996: 663). The main application Paul has in view here is doubtless the apostolic preaching of the gospel to the Jews. However, he frames the discussion in generalized terms and names neither himself as speaker nor Israel as addressee throughout vv. 5–18, indicating that the principles outlined here extend more widely to whenever and wherever the gospel is preached by commissioned agents.

through the gospel is not about doing, but rather about hearing and believing:

> But the righteousness based on faith says, 'Do not say in your heart, "Who will ascend into heaven?"' (that is, to bring Christ down) or '"Who will descend into the abyss?"' (that is, to bring Christ up from the dead). But what does it say? 'The word is near you, in your mouth and in your heart' (that is, the word of faith that we proclaim ['that we preach', *kēryssome*]) . . . (10:6–8)

In Deuteronomy 30:12–14 Moses tells the people of Israel that the commandment of God (which he has delivered to them) is not too difficult for them to keep. Here in Romans 10:6–8 Paul picks up on these words of Moses, but declares that the gospel does not require strenuous effort on the part of God's people to gain access to it. They do not need to reach up to heaven or down into the abyss to take hold of Christ, because he has descended to earth and been raised from the dead. That is to say, all that is needed to achieve salvation has been done already, and salvation is thus presented to humanity as a completed act through the preaching of the gospel. All that is required now is a believing response to the proclaimed word (10:9–13).

Paul has been at pains to demonstrate throughout Romans that the salvation announced in the gospel is, at its very heart, something that God achieves and that he gives to people, rather than something that sinful people achieve or attain for themselves. Here Paul shows that the dissemination of the gospel message through preaching reflects the very nature of the gospel as something given by God and received by humanity – in particular, *as something spoken to be heard*. Humanity does not need to seek out salvation, but the word of faith is near at hand through the preaching of the gospel (10:8), so that those in need of salvation need only hear, believe and confess.

Strikingly in this connection, Paul later draws upon the language of Isaiah 53:1 at Romans 10:16 (following the LXX) to label the preached message as 'the hearing'. Rendered literally, 10:16b reads: 'Lord, who has believed the hearing of us [*tē akoē hēmōn*]?' 'The hearing' in the context of Romans 10:16 (in line with its meaning in its original context in Isa. 53:1) refers to the preached message.[2] And

---

[2] The term *akoē* similarly means 'message' in the LXX of Isa. 52.7 ('like the feet of one bringing glad tidings of a report of peace', NETS). See the parallel use of the language of 'hearing' to refer to a preached message in 1 Thess. 2:13 and Heb. 4:2, and see our discussion of those verses below.

so when Paul says that 'faith comes from hearing [*ex akoēs*], and hearing [*hē akoē*] [comes] through the word of Christ' (10:17), he is playing on the language of 'hearing'.[3] He is at once picking up the term he has just used in the Isaiah quotation to refer to the sermon, while anticipating the same use of that language to designate the act of hearing through the physical organ of hearing in 10:18: 'But I ask, have they not heard [*ēkousan*]?'[4]

Preaching is by its very nature the declaration of a message that is designed to be heard. And since faith comes about through hearing the word of God, there is a fundamental correspondence between the act of preaching and the creation of faith. Paul is not simply suggesting that preaching is the best way of achieving the intended result of faith (as though his concern were merely pragmatic), but that preaching is *the* natural, appropriate and God-ordained means of producing faith, by its nature having a fundamental correspondence to the character of faith.

Christian preaching stands in a line of continuity with Old Testament prophetic proclamation

Through his appropriation of sections of Moses' great sermon in Deuteronomy 30 (especially vv. 12–14), Paul sets his own declaration of the gospel in a line of continuity with that great prophetic and authoritative declaration of God's word. At Deuteronomy 30:14 Moses says to the congregation in the wilderness that 'the word is very near you. It is in your mouth and in your heart, so that you can do it.' The context of this statement indicates that Moses is referring to the word of God that he has spoken to them: 'For this commandment that I command you today is not too hard for you, neither is it far off' (Deut. 30:11; see also vv. 15–16). In quoting Deuteronomy 30:14 at Romans 10:8, Paul replaces Moses with himself (and perhaps

---

[3] The range of meaning of *akoē* includes 'the faculty of hearing', 'the act of hearing', 'the organ w. which one hears' and 'that which is heard' (BDAG). Dunn (1988: 623), who takes the view that in v. 17 the term should be taken as 'the act of hearing', helpfully comments that '[w]hat seems unnatural to us because we have two different words ("report" and "hearing") would not seem so to the Greek hearer; the range of meaning of one and the same word is simply being exploited'.

[4] Whether in 10:17 Paul uses the term *akoē* to refer to preaching or to the act of hearing is not immediately clear and is a matter of debate (see brief discussion in Moo 1996: 665, fn. 27), but the difference is actually slight. In either case, the point is that faith comes through hearing the preached message. Whether the emphasis in v. 17 falls on the declaration itself ('preaching') or the reception ('the act of hearing') ultimately matters little.

the other apostles[5]) as the contemporary speaker of God's word: 'But what does it say? "The word is near you, in your mouth and in your heart" (that is, the word of faith that we proclaim).' Just as the Israelites in the wilderness were given God's word through Moses the great prophet and leader, so now the people of God are given his word through the apostle as representative Christian preacher.

In a similar vein, Paul sets the preaching ministry of Christian preachers within the framework of, and in a line of continuity with, that of the prophet Isaiah.[6] After outlining the necessity for preachers to be sent in order that others might hear the gospel (10:14–15a; verses to which we will return), he quotes from Isaiah 52:7 in 10:15b: 'How beautiful are the feet of those who preach [euangelizomenōn] the good news!'[7] In this verse Isaiah looks beyond his own ministry and anticipates the arrival of the messenger who will announce the ultimate salvation of God's people. The verse highlights the importance (even the 'beauty'[8]) of the proclamation of God's salvation. Further, 'it implicitly suggests that the last condition for salvation listed by Paul in vv. 14–15a has been met: God has sent preachers'.[9] In quoting this verse, Paul indicates that the proclamation of the gospel by Christian preachers fulfils the prophetic expectation of Isaiah for the messianic age.

In Romans 10:16, however, Paul goes a step further back, beyond Isaiah's prophetic expectations concerning future ministry, to Isaiah's own preaching ministry. Quoting Isaiah 53, Paul indicates that Christian preaching stands in a line of continuity with Isaiah's ministry: 'But they have not all obeyed the gospel. For Isaiah says, "Lord, who has believed what he has heard from us?"' Just as Isaiah's preaching met with a mixed response, so will contemporary Christian preaching. The Christian preacher stands with Isaiah as one who proclaims the word of God that leads to faith for those who will obey

---

[5] Paul does not specify the subjects of this first person plural verb. Probably the first person plural 'we proclaim' refers to Paul and the other apostles in the first instance. However, Paul never restricts the work of preaching to the apostles in this passage, and it is likely that he views himself here as a representative Christian preacher, rather than (specifically and exclusively) a representative apostle.

[6] At 10:14–18 Paul points all the more clearly beyond his own personal ministry. Although Paul still had his own preaching directly in view when he spoke of the 'word of faith that we proclaim' at 10:8, now the discussion is impersonal and general: 'And how are they to hear without someone preaching?' (10:14b).

[7] Note that the verbs kēryssō and euangelizomai are used interchangeably in 10:15.

[8] Although the term may rather indicate the 'timeliness' of this proclamation; see the lexical discussion in the commentaries.

[9] Moo 1996: 664.

the gospel (10:16–17).[10] The 'prophetic' character of the preached word underlies once again its authoritative nature. The proper response to the proclamation of the gospel is obedience (10:16a). However, as Isaiah found in his day, not all will respond in faith (10:16b).

Preaching rests upon and involves the action of Christ

Paul's theological reflections on preaching in these verses highlight the agency of Jesus in the preaching of the gospel at a number of points, not least in verse 14: 'How then will they call on him in whom they have not believed? And how are they to believe in him whom they have never heard?'[11] The verb *akouō* (to hear) usually takes the genitive case for its direct object when it is a person who is heard (rather than a thing, which can be in the accusative).[12] So, to see the genitive relative particle *hou* as the direct object of the verb is the more natural reading, '[i]n accordance with normal grammatical usage'.[13] Sanday and Headlam suggest that the relative particle *hou* here stands for *eis touton hou*, which 'means not "to hear of some one", but "to hear some one preaching or speaking"', and so they conclude that 'what follows must be interpreted by assuming that the preaching of Christ's messengers is identical with the preaching of Christ himself'.[14] As the preachers preach, Jesus is speaking.[15]

It is probably right to see a further indication of the agency of Jesus in the preaching of the gospel in Paul's summary verse, verse 17: 'So faith comes from hearing, and hearing through the word of Christ.' The genitive 'word *of Christ*' could indicate that the word comes from Christ (as its author or speaker) or that it concerns Christ (it is a word

---

[10] See Excursus 2 for other connections in the NT between Christian preachers and OT prophets.

[11] Here we follow the rendering offered in the ESV footnote, 'him whom they have never heard', rather than 'of whom'. Similarly, Cranfield 1985b: 262; Thayer 1896: 23; Stott 1994: 286; Morris 1988: 389–390; Dunn 1988: 620; Barrett 1991: 189. I am grateful to Tim Ward for drawing my attention to this point.

[12] BDAG, BDF § 173.

[13] Dunn 1988: 620. Interestingly, Thayer (1896: 23) finds that this verb 'is not joined with the genitive of the obj. unless one hear the person or thing with his own ears', which would imply that in this verse Christ himself is the one who must be heard.

[14] Sanday and Headlam 1920: 296.

[15] Given that Jesus' voice is heard through the preachers, it makes sense that the preachers should not be self-appointed, but must rather be commissioned to speak as his heralds (10:15). See further comments below.

'about Christ'). It is difficult to reach a firm conclusion on this point, and commentators differ. However, given what we have seen so far, the balance of the contextual evidence suggests that Paul intends the former – that faith comes through the word that Jesus speaks through the preachers he has sent.

Preaching requires a commission, but is not restricted to the apostles

Finally, it is significant to note again that, in Paul's presentation in this chapter, the commissioning of preachers is an essential prerequisite for their ministry. In his series of rhetorical questions outlining the conditions under which people can hear and respond to the gospel (10:14–15), his final question is, 'And how are they to preach unless they are sent?'

Here in the discussion of a commission to 'preach' (*kēryssō*) '[t]he image of the preacher/herald [*kēryx*] is implicit; fundamental to Paul's conception is the preacher as spokesman for another, not as someone with his own message authorized by himself'.[16] As we have already seen, Paul's use of Isaiah 52:7 presupposes that the Lord has commissioned and sent preachers of good news, in fulfilment of Isaiah's prophetic expectation. Paul's own commission came directly from Christ (1:4–5), and it seems most natural to understand him to mean that Jesus is the one who sends and commissions his preachers (cf. Eph. 4:11).[17] Here Paul is outlining the normal mechanism by which the gospel goes out, and it seems unavoidable to conclude that he expects the pattern of proclamation that leads to belief to be continually repeated throughout the church's age. These verses are not simply an apologia for Paul's own apostolic ministry, but a paradigm for how the gospel spreads. And in this paradigm for normal gospel ministry, those who proclaim good news are not self-selected mavericks, but rather are those who are commissioned and sent.[18]

---

[16] Dunn 1988: 621; so too Moo 1996: 663. See further comments on this point below.
[17] Kruse 2012: 217; Dunn 1988: 621.
[18] This corresponds with Paul's teaching in Eph. 4:11, where we learn that Jesus has given his church not only the foundational preachers of his word, 'the apostles and the prophets', but also those who continue that work in the post-apostolic period, 'the evangelists, the shepherds and teachers'.

Summary

In Romans 10 Paul establishes the central importance of preaching in God's plan of salvation for the world. The preached message, as a word that is proclaimed and heard, corresponds in a fundamental way to the gospel itself – a message of salvation that is freely given and intended simply to be received by faith. Gospel preaching stands in a line of continuity with Moses' and Isaiah's ministry, and fulfils the latter's prophetic expectation of the proclamation of good news in the messianic age. Jesus himself stands behind the authoritative preaching of his word, and he commissions preachers to do this vital work.

Chapter Six

1 Corinthians: The power of the gospel in authentic Christian preaching

The Corinthian Christians had evidently come to view Paul's preaching ministry as rhetorically deficient, and one key purpose of Paul's first Corinthian letter is to address those concerns and to defend the validity of his preaching.[1] Our interest in 1 Corinthians centres on chapters 1 – 2, 9 and 15. These chapters are of interest at a lexical level because all three of the 'semi-technical' preaching verbs that we have previously identified occur with some frequency in these sections (*euangelizomai*, 1:17; 9:16, 18; 15:1, 2; *kēryssō*, 1:23; 9:27; 15:11, 12; *katangellō*, 2:1; 9:14; see also 11:26), as do two of their cognates (*euangelion*, 4:15; 9:12, 14, 18, 23; 15:1; and *kērygma*, 1:21; 2:4; 15:14). Moreover, Paul's discussion of his preaching ministry in these chapters raises a number of matters relating to the nature of his preaching ministry (and Christian preaching in general) which are relevant for us. In the opening two chapters of the letter, Paul articulates and defends the character of his preaching ministry, comparing and contrasting it to contemporary rhetorical practice.[2] In chapter 9 he speaks of preachers as a distinct group of people within the church, and

[1] Litfin 2015: 132–172.
[2] Smith's (2012: 166–167) suggestion that the plural 'we preach' in 1:23 refers to 'Christians generally' rather than Paul (and possibly his associates) specifically is not persuasive. Paul brackets this discussion with clear reference to his commission from Christ to preach at Corinth (1:17) and a recollection of his initial coming (2:1). Quite clearly, throughout this section he is recalling his own earlier preaching ministry to the people at Corinth, maintaining a distinction between himself and his associates as proclaimers of the gospel and the believers at Corinth as recipients. He affirms the role of the Spirit in revealing the wisdom of God to him and the other apostles ('us') at 2:10–13, enabling him to impart those truths to the Corinthians. At 3:1–3 he recalls the fact that he, Paul, could not address the Corinthian believers ('you') as spiritual people when he first came. Paul maintains a distinction between himself (and his associates) and the church as a whole throughout chs. 3 and 4 (see esp. 3:9; 4:9–10). At the same time, Paul's use of the plural form of the first person rather than the singular is significant: it indicates that Paul is 'concerned to imply that such preaching is not unique to himself' (Fee 1987: 75, fn. 34).

considers the rights and obligations attached to their role. In chapter 15 he discusses the source and authority of authentic Christian preaching, as well as its expected results. The following exegetical observations are significant for our investigation.

Preaching is the central function of Paul's ministry in Corinth

In chapter 1 Paul speaks of a report he has received concerning divisions within the Corinthian church, with factions forming around key leaders (1:10–12). He says he is glad that he did not baptize many people at Corinth so that they could not claim their association with him through baptism as a basis for forming a clique around him (1:13–16). He goes on to affirm that his apostolic ministry at Corinth was not centred on baptism in any case, but rather on preaching: 'For Christ did not send me to baptize but to preach the gospel' (1:17). Paul's leadership and authority were centred on a preaching ministry in Corinth, and not on other ministry tasks. 'Whatever else may be said about Paul's ministry [at Corinth and elsewhere], at the behavioural level public speaking is what he actually did . . . Paul's ministry was singularly focused on his role as a public speaker.'[3] Paul explains why his ministry had this priority: the preached 'word of the cross', he affirms, 'is the power of God' (1:18).[4]

Preaching is distinct from other forms of oratory in its style and source of 'power'

It seems likely that the Corinthians were impressed by other contemporary orators and the secular wisdom they taught, and so questioned whether Paul's preaching offered the final word on 'wisdom' or represented a true expression of 'power' (whether rhetorical, intellectual or spiritual).[5] In addressing such perceived objections, Paul compares his preaching with other forms of oratory. This comparison is implicit throughout 1:18–31, where he contrasts the 'wisdom of the world'

[3] Litfin 2015: 133.
[4] The phrase 'the word of the cross' 'suggests both the content of the communication and the act of proclamation, just as "word" in English can mean both what is said and the act of speaking; "proclamation of the cross" captures the two dimensions' (Ciampa and Rosner 2010: 90).
[5] The other orators in question may include already the 'super-apostles' Paul speaks of in 2 Cor. 10 – 13, although this is not certain. See Lim 1987.

(1:20) and the 'wisdom' that Greeks seek (1:22) with the message he preaches, that is, 'Christ crucified' (1:23). A contrast between Paul's preaching and the rhetoric the Corinthians prized is strongly implicit in 1:17–25 and comes closer to the surface in 2:1–5, where Paul comments directly on his own 'rhetorical' (or perhaps better, 'anti-rhetorical') method:

> And I, when I came to you, brothers, did not come proclaiming [*katangellōn*] to you the testimony of God with lofty speech or wisdom. For I decided to know nothing among you except Jesus Christ and him crucified. And I was with you in weakness and in fear and much trembling, and my speech and my message [*kērygma*] were not in plausible words of wisdom, but in demonstration of the Spirit and of power, that your faith might not rest in the wisdom of men but in the power of God.

The 'lofty speech' and 'words of wisdom' Paul refers to here almost certainly characterize the rhetoric of other preachers in Corinth whose preaching the Corinthian Christians found attractive. His character-ization of the methods he rejects in his preaching suggests that these other preachers adopted patterns of oratory and rhetoric derived from secular Graeco-Roman practice. Paul insists that the power of his preaching comes not from these worldly techniques, but from the gospel message itself.[6]

The character of this worldly rhetoric and the precise feature(s) of it that Paul repudiates are debated.[7] A thorough evaluation of the various proposals is beyond the scope of this study, but we can none-theless note two basic points that are significant for our purposes. First, the contrast Paul draws between his preaching and worldly rhetoric indicates that his preaching is a form of public speaking capable of comparison at a basic level with the public speaking of others in Corinth who employ tools of rhetoric and oratory. When Paul speaks of 'preaching' in these chapters, he clearly means public proclamation.

Second, the contrast Paul draws between himself and contemporary

---

[6] Lim 1987: 145–149; Smith 2012: 172–173.

[7] A number of major studies have sought to identify the rhetorical practice or approach that Paul sought to distance himself from in 1 Corinthians. Two of the most significant studies in recent years are those of Litfin (2015), who affirms that Paul repudiated the central function of rhetoric itself, which he identifies as persuasion; and Winter (2002), who argues that Paul repudiated the ornamental and deceptive rhetorical practice of the contemporary Sophists.

rhetoricians establishes a central characteristic of his preaching: its divine source of 'power'. Paul's discussion of the nature of his own preaching in contrast to the expectations of the Corinthians and the practice of other orators is bracketed by mention of 'power' at 1:17b and 2:5, indicating the centrality of the idea of 'power' to the discourse at this point. In the Graeco-Roman world the term 'power' was often 'associated with rhetoric and eloquence, for orators could expect to win fame and glory'.[8] Paul's proclamation, however, derives its 'power' and effectiveness not from the rhetorical techniques employed or Paul's own skill as a speaker, but from the message itself and the work of the Spirit. The preaching of the gospel is powerful only because it is an expression of the 'power of God'.[9] Paul thus indicates that God himself stands behind the activity of proclamation as its ultimate agent.[10] Rather than being a rhetorician whose power lies in his skill, Paul is a herald whose power lies in his message and stems from the God who commissioned him to preach.

God is the source of our power in preaching

Preachers have a specific identity and role within the church, carrying particular rights and obligations

In 1 Corinthians 9, Paul speaks about the 'rights' that he has foregone in preaching the gospel in Corinth, including his right to material support. Paul's defence against the claims of the 'super-apostles' in 2 Corinthians 10 – 12 indicates that part of the criticism ultimately levelled against him at Corinth was that he seemed weak and inferior in comparison with these other preachers (see 2 Cor. 10:1, 10–12; 11:5–6). A purported mark of his weakness was that he did not charge for his preaching (2 Cor. 11:7–11). In 1 Corinthians 9, however, Paul wants to make it clear that he had every right to claim material support from the Corinthians when he preached the gospel to them, even though he forewent those rights for the sake of the gospel. He develops

8 Ciampa and Rosner 2010: 88. See further ref. there to the work of P. Marshall.

9 As Ciampa and Rosner (2010: 90) rightly note (in evaluation of Litfin's proposal in particular): 'Paul's stress seems to fall on the unconventional and value-inverting nature of the gospel message. It is not that he does not try to persuade, but he trusts in God's power working through him and his message rather than trusting in his own powers of persuasion, knowing that *the message of the cross*, despite seeming foolish, has divine power that other messages lack' (italics in original).

10 Smith 2012: 177.

this argument in 9:1–14, drawing parallels between gospel preachers and workers in other spheres.

Having affirmed that he and Barnabas should be free from having to earn their own living, Paul compares their situation with that of a soldier and a farmer: 'Who serves as a soldier at his own expense? Who plants a vineyard without eating any of its fruit? Or who tends a flock without getting some of the milk?' (9:7). He traces the principle back to the Old Testament law, drawing on Deuteronomy 25:4 in verse 9, and again establishes parallels between the world of agriculture (the work of the ploughman and the thresher) and the activity of preaching (9:8–12). Drawing a conceptually more proximate parallel from the world of religious service, Paul compares their situation with the situation of those who serve in the temple: 'Do you not know that those who are employed in the temple service get their food from the temple, and those who serve at the altar share in the sacrificial offerings?' (9:13).

Having established the principle that workers rightly expect to be paid, Paul applies the principle to himself and Barnabas in their work as preachers. In doing so, Paul does not limit the application of this principle to Barnabas and himself, but rather generalizes its application to all who preach the gospel. Moreover, he insists that the principle goes back to the Lord Jesus himself: 'In the same way, the Lord commanded that those who proclaim the gospel [*to euangelion katangellousin*] should get their living by the gospel' (9:14). Paul treats preaching the gospel as a type of work comparable to military service, farming or temple service. This type of work requires a level of dedication that merits material support. Further, the activity of preaching is sufficiently characteristic of the people who undertake the work that they can be treated as their own group, identified as 'those who preach the gospel'. The generalization of the principle Paul establishes, alongside the inclusion of Barnabas in the application of the principle, indicates that it applies beyond the apostolic office to others who preach. Paul's statement in 9:14 (which probably refers to the instruction of Jesus recorded in Luke 10:7; cf. Matt. 10:7–10) 'suggests continuity with the didactic ministry of Jesus' disciples and indicates the existence of a recognised group in the early Christian movement whose responsibility it was to proclaim the gospel'.[11]

This rightful expectation of material support is a privilege tied to the role of the preacher. However, Paul indicates that the role also

---

[11] Smith 2012: 195.

carries significant obligation and responsibility. 'Necessity' is laid upon him because he has been 'entrusted with a stewardship' (9:17), that is, to preach the gospel. The weight of stewardship on Paul's shoulders in preaching the gospel is nothing less than the salvation of others (9:22). Knowing that responsibility, Paul cries out, 'Woe to me if I do not preach the gospel!' (9:16).[12]

Christian preaching is the delivery of the received gospel of Christ

Discussion of a 'stewardship' in 1 Corinthians 9 highlights the fact that the gospel Paul preached was a message he had received, and so his role was to pass it on faithfully. As a steward, he was prepared to forego his rights, not for the sake of his personal reputation, but so that the gospel itself would not be hindered. Paul was willing to 'endure anything rather than put an obstacle in the way of the gospel of Christ' (9:12). This conviction of his responsibility as a steward was evident earlier in the letter when Paul closely aligned his message with 'the cross of Christ' (1:17) and affirmed that he had resolved in his preaching to 'know nothing among you except Jesus Christ and him crucified' (2:2). This theme of faithfulness to the received gospel comes to the fore when Paul returns to discuss his own preaching in chapter 15.

Paul reminds the Corinthians of 'the gospel I preached [*euēngelisamēn*] to you, which you received, in which you stand, and by which you are being saved, if you hold fast to the word I preached [*euēngelisamēn*] to you' (15:1–2). His preaching consisted essentially of the message he had received: 'For I delivered to you as of first importance what I also received: that Christ died for our sins in accordance with the Scriptures, that he was buried, that he was raised on the third day in accordance with the Scriptures' (15:3–5). As a preacher, his job was to 'testify' accurately to what he had received from Christ, and by no

---

[12] Aernie (2012: 73–90) argues that here in 1 Cor. 9:15–18 Paul's presentation of the obligation he bears as a preacher of the gospel recalls similar treatments of the prophetic office in various OT books. In particular, he finds that the notion of divine constraint (9:17) recalls Jeremiah's compulsion to proclaim the Lord's word (Jer. 20:7–10) and the 'woe-formula' of 9:16 recalls formulas associated with the commission of Isaiah and Jeremiah (Isa. 6:5; Jer. 15:10). Although Aernie's case is not conclusive at this point (the specific intertextual links he finds with Isaiah and Jeremiah here in 1 Cor. 9 are suggestive rather than concrete), it certainly resonates with our earlier findings that Paul presents himself and his ministry as standing in a line of continuity with the prophetic office in the OT.

means to 'misrepresent' him (see 15:15). If Paul's practice is to be taken as a model, then Christian preaching is fundamentally nothing more and nothing less than an accurate transmission of the received gospel of the sin-bearing death and resurrection of Christ.[13]

Preaching requires a believing response and leads to salvation

Paul attaches great significance to the preaching of this received word and to the hearers' response to it. The Corinthians 'are being saved' by the preached word, but only 'if you hold fast to the word I preached to you' (15:2). To question or deny the faithfully preached word is incomprehensible to Paul: 'Now if Christ is proclaimed as raised from the dead, how can some of you say that there is no resurrection of the dead?' (15:12). The faithful proclamation of this received word should be sufficient to put doubt to rest and precludes legitimate contradiction. Ultimately, the response – and continued response – to this preached word is a matter of life and death.

Summary

As Paul defends his preaching ministry in Corinth, he presents preaching as the central activity of his apostolic ministry. At the same time, he characterizes preaching as a more generalized class of work, exercised by a group of people that includes him and Barnabas, but extending beyond them as well. It is a type of work that merits material support and the dedication of the worker's time, while placing an obligation of serious stewardship upon the worker. The steward's obligation is to proclaim what he has received: the true message of Christ's sin-bearing death and resurrection. The proclamation of this message brings salvation and requires a believing response. Throughout this presentation and defence of his ministry of public gospel proclamation in Corinth, Paul uses interchangeably the three semi-technical terms for preaching, thus confirming our earlier suggestion that the three terms regularly function synonymously with the semi-technical meaning 'to preach'.[14]

---

[13] As Litfin (2015: 185) rightly points out, Paul viewed himself primarily as a herald whose 'task was to convey as faithfully as possible the already-constituted message of the author. He was simply an agent, a messenger.'

[14] See Smith 2012: 182.

Chapter Seven

2 Corinthians 2 – 6: Beholding the glory of God in preaching

The whole of 2 Corinthians is rich in its teaching on the nature of gospel ministry and the subject of preaching is never far from view throughout the letter. However, for the sake of brevity, we will restrict our analysis primarily to 2:12 – 6:13, where Paul addresses most directly his (and his associates') preaching ministry. From this section we can make the following eight key observations.

Paul is reflecting on the nature of new-covenant ministry

In the background to 2 Corinthians is a challenge to Paul's ministry from the so-called 'super-apostles' whom the Corinthian believers are tempted to believe and follow, but who peddle a distorted gospel (2 Cor. 11:4–6). As in 1 Corinthians, a major sub-theme of the letter is the authenticity of Paul's apostolic ministry (and the corresponding authenticity of the ministry of his associates, especially Timothy and Silas). This theme emerges in the opening chapters, where Paul speaks of their integrity and the authenticity of their message (1:12–14), where he affirms that (unlike others) they have been 'commissioned by God' (2:17), and where he raises the question of whether they need to 'commend' themselves before the Corinthians (3:1–6). Within that broader context, Paul then reflects specifically on the nature of the ministry that has been entrusted to him and to his associates in 2:12 – 6:13. Presumably he does this, at least in part, in order to educate the Corinthians as to the true nature of all authentic new-covenant ministry (and not simply his own) so that they might be able to recognize and continue to receive such ministry.

The ministry he has in view is a shared ministry

Although Paul's own apostolic ministry is especially in view in this section of 2 Corinthians, the focus is not exclusively on Paul. The letter is signed by both Paul and Timothy (1:1).[1] As Paul reflects specifically on his time ministering in Corinth, he speaks not only of his own proclamation of the gospel, but of the proclamation of Timothy and Silas (or Silvanus) as well (see Acts 18:5). Indeed, Paul seems to be at pains to highlight the fact that the preaching of the gospel at Corinth was done not simply by him, but by his associates as well: 'For the Son of God, Jesus Christ, whom we proclaimed among you, *Silvanus and Timothy and I*, was not Yes and No, but in him it is always Yes' (1:19). And so Paul's frequent use of the first person plural ('we', 'us') indicates, at least at some points within the letter (in particular, at 1:19 and following), that he is speaking for Timothy and Silas.[2] This observation is confirmed by Paul's description of himself and his associates as 'ministers [or 'servants'] of a new covenant' (3:6; see also 6:4). Rather than refer to himself as he frequently does using the title 'apostle', which points to his authoritative office, here Paul uses a term that points to his and his associates' 'activity of service'. Unlike the title 'apostle', 'Paul can share this title with those who are also engaged in the proclamation of the gospel'.[3] The fact that Paul's ministry of proclamation is a shared ministry is significant for our thinking, because it means that the lessons we glean here about the nature of new-covenant ministry are not only applicable to Paul the apostle; they carry forward beyond the apostolic office.[4]

[1] The exact nature of Timothy's involvement in the production of the letter is not spelled out and is the subject of some debate among commentators. The mention of Timothy at 1:1 most probably represents the fact that Timothy shared with Paul in the ministry at Corinth (see Acts 18:5; 1 Cor. 4:17; and 2 Cor. 1:19), has an ongoing pastoral concern for the Corinthians, and stands alongside him in affirming the substance of the letter (Harris 2005: 131).

[2] So Cranfield 1985a: 224. Throughout the section 2 Cor. 1:15–24 'there appears to be a very careful distinction between singular and plural' (Moule 1963: 119), indicating that where the plural is used in that section, it is intended to indicate that Paul is speaking for himself and his associates. However, it is uncertain that this is the case consistently throughout the letter; at least some of the instances of the first person plural may simply be authorial plurals. For further discussion see Thrall 1994: 105–107; and Barnett 1997: 58, esp. fn. 7.

[3] Hafemann 2005: 111. Although Hafemann highlights the inclusive nature of the term, note that he believes that in the use of the term here at 2 Cor. 3:6 Paul is referring only to himself.

[4] So, rightly, Adam 1996: 81: 'In 2 Corinthians . . . Paul paints a picture of his own ministry as an example for other Christian ministers. In saying that God "has made us competent to be ministers of a new covenant" (3:6), Paul is describing not only his own

The particular ministry he has in view is a ministry of public proclamation

As Paul looks back at the ministry that he, Timothy and Silas have exercised in Corinth, he describes it as a ministry of proclamation: 'For the Son of God, Jesus Christ, whom we proclaimed [*kēryxtheis*] among you . . .' (1:19). Here Paul refers to his activity at Corinth using the verb *kēryssō*, which, as we have seen, regularly designates the public proclamation of the gospel by authoritative agents in the New Testament.[5] To see the verb as bearing this meaning here certainly coheres with the immediate context. Paul's description of the effect of their ministry and the response it evokes in the people of God suggests a setting in congregational worship, which would of course be a natural setting for the public proclamation of the gospel. Having mentioned the proclamation of the gospel in verse 19, Paul recalls the church's corporate response in verse 20: 'That is why it is through him that we utter our Amen to God for his glory.'[6] Reflecting briefly on his ministry in Troas, Paul likewise presents that ministry as consisting centrally of preaching. His express purpose in going there was 'to preach' (2:12).[7] 'That he actually did proclaim the good news in Troas is a fair inference from the following reference to an "open door", for this "door" would be recognized to be "open" only after he had grasped the opportunities for preaching.'[8]

At 2:14–17 Paul moves away from specific reflection on his time in

ministry as an apostle but also that of all who join with him in preaching the apostolic gospel. He repeatedly outlines the style of his ministry not only to explain to the Corinthians why they ought to believe the gospel he has given them, but also to encourage them to exercise a comparable ministry.'

[5] Paul will again describe their ministry in Corinth using the verb *kēryssō* as he sets it in contrast to that of false apostles: 'For if someone comes and proclaims another Jesus than the one we proclaimed . . .' (11:4). Barnett rightly notes of the use of this verb here that it is a 'solemn verb' and bears the meaning 'proclaimed as by a herald' (Barnett 1997: 105).

[6] Cf. 1 Cor. 14:16. 'The context of the church at worship is clear from 1 Cor 14 . . . and it may well be traced here' (Martin 1986: 27). Barnett similarly detects a context of corporate worship here: 'Again we see a connection between the church's praise of God and the apostolic proclamation . . . The words of the church's worship echo back to God that gospel word through which the church has its existence. Speaking for God and from God the apostle proclaimed the Son of God . . . God's great "Yes"; the messianic assembly, gathered by that word, answers with its "Amen", to the glory of God through Jesus Christ' (Barnett 1997: 109; so, too, Harris 2005: 204).

[7] As the ESV translates it reasonably in context, although the Greek is less concrete (*eis to euangelion*).

[8] Harris 2005: 237.

Corinth, Troas or Macedonia, and turns to consider more generally the nature of the ministry that he (and probably his associates; note the transition back to the first person plural) has been given. Again, this ministry is presented as both public in its context and verbal in its nature. Paul points to the public context of this ministry through the evocative imagery he uses of being led by Christ in a 'triumphal procession' which 'spreads the fragrance of the knowledge of him everywhere' (2:14). Verse 14 does not specify the means by which 'the fragrance of the knowledge of [Christ]' is disseminated, but verse 17 makes it clear that this communication was irreducibly verbal in nature, indicating that Paul's preaching ministry has remained in view in these verses: 'For we are not, like so many, peddlers of God's word, but as men of sincerity, as commissioned by God, in the sight of God we speak in Christ.'[9]

In chapter 3 Paul proceeds to describe the nature of the new-covenant ministry entrusted to him and his associates, setting it in contrast to old-covenant ministry. This new-covenant ministry is a ministry of the Spirit that comes with more 'glory' than the ministry of 'death', which was 'carved in letters on stone' (3:7–11). In developing the contrast between new-covenant ministry and old-covenant ministry, Paul sets his and his associates' ministry against the backdrop of two particular instances or modes of old-covenant ministry. The first is that exercised by Moses at Sinai (recalling Exod. 34), where, having met with the Lord and having received the law, Moses descended from the mountain and proceeded to speak to the people, covering his face with a veil (2 Cor. 3:12–14; see Exod. 34:29–35). This pattern was then repeated whenever Moses went into the sanctuary in the tabernacle to meet with God and then 'came out and told the people of Israel what he was commanded' (Exod. 34:34). The second mode of old-covenant ministry in view is the reading (and presumably preaching) of the law in the temple and in synagogues (2 Cor. 3:14–15).

The significant observation for our present purposes is that in both these modes of old-covenant ministry, the implied context is the public proclamation of God's word to the gathered assembly of God's people, first in the wilderness at Sinai and at the tabernacle (3:7, 13),

---

[9] The witness of Paul's sacrificial life and ministry, following the example of Jesus, is almost certainly in view here as well. However, the witness of Paul's life cannot be separated from his proclamation of Christ; indeed, it would not serve to disseminate 'knowledge of him' (v. 14) without being accompanied by verbal proclamation. See the detailed analysis of Hafemann (2000a: 35–83, and note esp. 47) alongside discussion in the commentaries.

then at the temple and the synagogue (3:14–15).[10] Thus a key basis of Paul's comparison and contrast here between old-covenant ministry and the ministry in which he and his associates have been engaged is a common public context – specifically, the context of the assembly of God's people.[11] '[T]his ministry' (4:1), which consists of 'the open statement of the truth' (4:2), is a ministry of proclamation: 'For what we proclaim [kēryssomen] is not ourselves, but Jesus Christ as Lord' (4:5).

The ministry of proclamation is grounded in Scripture

As Paul compares and contrasts new-covenant ministry with old-covenant ministry, a key point of commonality is the basis of both ministries in the revelation of God. Moses encountered God at Sinai and received God's word (the law) to give to the people. Throughout the subsequent generations of old-covenant ministry, that ministry was grounded in the reading of the old-covenant Scriptures (3:14), that is, the reading of 'Moses' (3:15). The difference Paul highlights between new-covenant and old-covenant ministry is not the basis of revelation in the Scriptures, but rather the ability of God's people to perceive what is found in Scripture. Now under the new covenant the 'the veil is removed' through Christ (3:16), and so God's people can behold Christ in his glory when the scriptural word is proclaimed.

---

[10] Martin (1986: 68, 73), Barnett (1997: 194) and Thrall (1994: 263–267) similarly see the implied context in vv. 14 and 15 as being Sabbath synagogue worship. The reading and preaching of the Scriptures was a key component of the synagogue meeting: 'For from ancient generations Moses has had in every city those who proclaim [kēryssontas] him, for he is read every Sabbath in the synagogues' (Acts 15:21). See also the ancient synagogue inscription at Jerusalem signed by Theodotus son of Vettenus, which affirms that the purpose of the synagogue was 'for the reading of the law and the teaching of the commandments'. This pattern is reflected in Paul and Barnabas' visit to the synagogue in Pisidian Antioch: 'After the reading from the Law and the Prophets, the rulers of the synagogue sent a message to them, saying, "Brothers, if you have any word of encouragement for the people, say it"' (Acts 13:15). The term 'word of encouragement' (logos paraklēseōs) is a term used to designate a sermon (see the writer of Hebrews' use of the term to designate his written sermon at Heb. 13:22 and our discussion of Hebrews as a sermon later in this present volume).

[11] The fact that Paul should draw such a comparison is quite natural, given that the Christian practice of meeting to hear the reading and proclamation of God's word almost certainly evolved out of the synagogue meeting. In this connection see Beckwith 2003: 28–54.

The clear implication is that the ministry remains grounded in the same Scriptures.

God the Trinity is at work in the ministry of proclamation

As Paul and his ministry associates engage in this ministry of public proclamation of God's word, Paul believes that God the Trinity is powerfully at work. Indeed, at certain points he implies strongly that this ministry of preaching is fundamentally something that God himself does in and through his agents.

In his reflection on his preaching ministry with Silas and Timothy in Corinth at 2 Corinthians 1:19, Paul uses what is almost certainly a divine passive of the verb 'preach' to point to the fact that it was ultimately God who was the preacher:[12] 'For the Son of God, Jesus Christ, who was preached among you by us – by me, Silas [or 'Silvanus'] and Timothy – was not "Yes" and "No", but in him it has always been "Yes".'[13] Paul then highlights God's agency explicitly as he describes what God has achieved as his word has been proclaimed: 'And it is God who establishes us with you in Christ, and has anointed us, and who has also put his seal on us and given us his Spirit in our hearts as a guarantee' (1:21–22).[14]

Later in chapter 2, in the verses already noted above, Paul gives thanks *for what God has achieved* through his and his associates' ministry: 'But thanks be to God, who in Christ always leads us in triumphal procession, and through us spreads the fragrance of the knowledge of him everywhere' (2:14). He asks who can be sufficient for such a role (2:16), and answers that he and his associates can be sufficient because they have been 'commissioned by God' and 'in the sight of God we speak in Christ' (2:17). In both 2:14 and 2:17 Paul speaks of the ministry – which is quite beyond human sufficiency – as

---

[12] Barnett 1997: 106.

[13] Here we follow the NIV, which renders this more literally than the ESV.

[14] Barnett rightly relates the action of God by his Spirit in vv. 21b–22 to the preaching of Christ in v. 20: 'God's ongoing action toward his people guaranteeing ['establishes us', v. 21a ESV] their Christward focus rests upon and is in contrast to a single complete action (which is here stated as three closely connected actions, each involving the Spirit). That single complete action of God corresponds to the action of the apostolic proclamation of the Son of God in Corinth. Paul "preached" Christ, and the hearers were "anointed" by the Spirit' (Barnett 1997: 111). Note that not only the preaching of the word but also the congregation's response to the word is achieved in and through God's enabling: 'That is why it is through him [that is, through Christ] that we utter our Amen to God for his glory' (1:20).

being achieved 'in Christ' before God the Father, meaning in union with Christ by his Spirit, and enabled by Christ.

At the start of chapter 3 Paul asks where their commendation for ministry comes from, and he answers that God has made the Corinthians themselves a letter of recommendation (3:1–2). He continues, 'And you show that you are a letter from Christ, delivered by us [lit. 'ministered by us'], written not with ink but with the Spirit of the living God, not on tablets of stone but on tablets of human hearts' (3:3). As Paul and his associates have ministered faithfully by proclaiming the message of Christ, Christ by the Spirit of God has been at work transforming hearts. Paul insists that he can take no credit for this: 'Not that we are sufficient in ourselves to claim anything as coming from us, but our sufficiency is from God, who has made us competent to be ministers of a new covenant' (3:5–6).

This dynamic sheds light on the curious fact that, as Paul goes on to describe the nature of the new-covenant ministry that they are engaged in, he presents himself and his associates not simply as agents of the ministry (it is certainly their ministry of proclamation that remains in view, as 4:1–5 makes clear), but also as recipients of the ministry of the Spirit:

> Now the Lord is the Spirit, and where the Spirit of the Lord is, there is freedom. And we all, with unveiled face, beholding the glory of the Lord, are being transformed into the same image from one degree of glory to another. For this comes from the Lord who is the Spirit. (3:17–18)

As Paul, Timothy and Silas proclaim the new covenant in the power of the Spirit, they themselves become recipients, along with God's assembled people ('we all', 3:18), of the transforming ministry of the Spirit. This is only possible because in the ministry of new-covenant proclamation, the primary actor is not the preacher, but God himself.

Paul attests that God has graciously taught him that lesson and kept him mindful of it through bringing adversity into his experience:

> But we have this treasure [referring to the message of Jesus Christ as Lord that they proclaim, 4:5] in jars of clay, to show that the surpassing power belongs to God and not to us . . . always carrying in the body the death of Jesus, so that the life of Jesus may also be manifested in our bodies. For we who live are always being given

over to death for Jesus' sake, so that the life of Jesus also may be manifested in our mortal flesh. (4:7–11)

The fruit of this adversity is the manifestation of the life of Jesus through the ministry Paul and his associates carry out.

Paul again emphasizes the primary agency of God in their preaching ministry when he describes them as being 'ambassadors for Christ, God making his appeal through us' (5:20), as they 'work together' with God (6:1).

The glory of God is revealed in the ministry of proclamation

A central feature of the contrast Paul develops between Moses' old-covenant ministry and his own new-covenant ministry is the differing degree to which God's glory is manifested through those ministries. Moses' ministry did come with a limited glory (3:7, 10), which was reflected in Moses' glowing (and promptly veiled) face (3:7, 13). In the case of new-covenant ministry, however, the veil is taken away and there is now 'freedom' for God's people to 'behold' the 'glory of the Lord' (3:16–18). In speaking of 'glory' Paul refers to the glory of God himself which is revealed as he is encountered in the ministry of his servants in the two covenants. The greater 'glory' attending the ministry of the new covenant suggests a more open and direct encounter with the Lord in his glory than the people of God were able to experience under the old covenant.

The contrast between new-covenant and old-covenant ministry – and between Paul and Moses as covenant ministers[15] – is centrally

---

[15] So Martin (1986: 6) and Thrall (1994: 254), but *contra* Barnett (1997: 190, esp. fn. 4), who maintains that in 3:12–18 Paul's first person plural references do not refer to himself with respect to his ministry, but rather more generally as a representative of all new-covenant people. However, the initial point of contrast is not between the Israelites and the new-covenant people, but quite clearly between Paul and Moses (vv. 12–13). Referring back to the substance of these verses, Paul speaks of 'having this ministry' (4:1), by which he must mean a new-covenant ministry that stands both in parallel with, and in contrast to, that of Moses. Of course, as argued above, as Paul and his associates minister under the new covenant through the proclamation of the word, they themselves become recipients of the word and so stand alongside all new-covenant people in receiving the ministry and beholding God's glory. Harris' summary is judicious: '3:12–18 incorporates contrasts between two ministries, two covenants, and two religions. It ends (in v. 18) with contrasts that are partly explicit and partly implicit, between two sets of persons, Moses and the Jews on the one hand, and Paul and Christians on the other. Under the new covenant, not one man alone, but all Christians behold and then reflect the glory of the Lord' (Harris 2005: 318).

developed at 3:12–18, and it will be helpful to trace Paul's flow of logic in these verses in some detail. As we have seen already, Paul has been considering the nature and authority of his preaching ministry in the opening chapters of the letter, and that focus continues and remains central in these verses.[16] When Moses addressed the people in the wilderness, he put a veil over his face to keep the Israelites from gazing 'at the outcome of what was being brought to an end' (3:13). In the reflected glory of his shining face, Moses showed something of the glory of God that would be revealed fully in the gospel (see 4:4), which was the final 'outcome' and fulfilment of the old covenant that was 'coming to an end'. Beyond Moses' day, a veil (now covering their minds) continues to prevent the people of Israel from seeing the glory of God in the old-covenant word because 'their minds were hardened' (3:14–15). Unlike Moses, however, Paul is 'very bold' (3:12). The term translated 'bold' here is the Greek term *parrēsia*, which carries the sense of liberty, openness and boldness in speech. Paul's liberty in preaching the gospel contrasts with Moses' guardedness in putting a veil over his face when communicating the old covenant.

Having contrasted his own ministry with that of Moses, Paul then reflects on the difference in experience between new-covenant people and old-covenant people as they receive the ministry of God's word. For Christians who have turned to 'the Lord' (that is, the Lord Jesus)[17] 'the veil is removed' (3:16). And the result of the removal of the veil is 'liberty' or 'freedom' effected by the Spirit (3:17), who makes it possible for the people of God to behold the Lord in his glory: 'And we all, with unveiled face, beholding the glory of the Lord, are being transformed into the same image, from one degree of glory to another. For this comes from the Lord who is the Spirit' (3:18). When the Spirit of God is at work as the gospel is proclaimed under the new covenant, there is 'freedom', not only for the new-covenant minister to speak with 'liberty' and 'boldness' (3:12) of Christ in all his glory, but also for the listening people to behold the glory of the Lord. The wonder of new-covenant ministry when set against the old-covenant ministry of Moses is that now, by the Spirit

---

[16] '3:12–18 is no independent section, loosely appended to chap. 3, but integral to it.' In these verses Paul's focus continues to be 'his preaching ministry, its authority and effectiveness' (Martin 1986: 66). Martin notes the large number of verbal links ('impressive in number and significance') between this section and the preceding and following sections of the letter, reinforcing their close connection to one another.

[17] Here Paul probably reflects on his own experience as a Jew turning to Christ on the Damascus Road.

of God, it is possible to behold the glory of God as his word is proclaimed.[18]

Paul refers again to this privilege in 4:4–6. He notes that some will fail to see the glory of Christ in his preaching, but only because 'the god of this world has blinded the minds of the unbelievers, to keep them from seeing the light of the gospel of the glory of Christ, who is the image of God' (4:4). Unbelievers are blinded because of the god of this world, but otherwise they would see the glory of Christ (and so the image of God) in the preaching of the gospel. Reminding the Corinthians that 'we proclaim . . . Jesus Christ as Lord, with ourselves as your servants for Jesus' sake' (4:5), Paul explains why he preaches: 'For God, who said, "Let light shine out of darkness", has shone in our hearts to give the light of the knowledge of the glory of God in the face of Jesus Christ' (4:6). That is, God in his mercy has revealed his glory to Paul (on the Damascus Road), and so Paul preaches as a servant of the people of God. By implication, Paul does this in order that through his preaching and by the mercy of God others might experience the same miracle of understanding ('the knowledge of') the gospel that leads to beholding 'the glory of God in the face of Jesus Christ'.

The people of God are transformed through the ministry of proclamation

In turning to Christ, the veil is removed (3:18) so that people are at liberty to behold the Lord as his word is proclaimed (3:17). The implication of this is that the proclamation of Christ from the word of God entails a transformative encounter with the Lord himself: 'And we all, with unveiled face, beholding the glory of the Lord, are being transformed into the same image from one degree of glory to another. For this comes from the Lord who is the Spirit' (3:18). An encounter with the Lord Jesus Christ ('who is the image of God', 4:4b) results in his people being 'transformed into the same image' in increasing degrees of glory. Even under the old covenant there was an extent to

---

[18] Hafemann (2005: 425) similarly locates the 'encounter' with the glory of God as happening in and through the preaching of the gospel: 'But where and how does this encounter with the glory of God take place for Paul? Although Paul does not deal with this question directly in the passage before us, the answer is certainly presupposed in the matter of fact way in which Paul introduces the concept in 3:18 and 4:4–6, and in his reference to his own boldness in ministry in 3:12. These texts give the most immediate answer, namely, in the preaching of the Gospel of Jesus Christ.'

which this happened for Moses. When he encountered the Lord in his glory, his face shone for a time as he reflected something of the glory of God. However, the fruit of the divine encounter was limited for Moses, and, because of the veil, this encounter was not shared with the whole company of God's people. But the 'freedom' of the new covenant in Christ means that, as his word is proclaimed by his servant (initially Paul in this context), the encounter with God is unrestricted. Thus the fruit of the encounter through the proclaimed word is radical, Spirit-enabled transformation of the people of God into the likeness of Christ.

New-covenant preaching ministry has affinities to old-covenant prophetic ministry

We have already noted and examined Paul's sustained comparison (at 3:12–18) of the old-covenant ministry of Moses and the new-covenant ministry of proclamation in which Paul and his associates are engaged. Although much of what Paul highlights is contrastive, there are key elements of correspondence between his ministry and the ministry of Moses that underlie the comparison: both ministries were grounded in God's word, both took place in a public setting, both were ministries of proclamation, and both reflected something of the glory of God. These points of correspondence provide a basis for the comparison Paul undertakes. A further point of correspondence is probably to be found at 2:16, where Paul asks rhetorically who is 'sufficient' for the ministry entrusted to him and his associates. Along with a number of scholars, Hafemann plausibly maintains that

> [t]he language of 'sufficiency' used here alludes to the call of Moses in Exodus 4:10, where in the LXX Moses responds to God's call by declaring that he is not 'sufficient' (*hikanos*) for the task of speaking on the Lord's behalf. In the context of Exodus 4, Moses is *made sufficient* by God himself. Paul too sees his sufficiency as coming from God (cf. 2 Cor. 3:4–6).[19]

This verbal resonance with LXX Exodus 4:10 would not on its own establish the suggestion that Paul intended an allusion to Moses' call, but the explicit comparison of himself and Moses that follows at

---

[19] Hafemann 2000b: 113 (italics in original).

3:12–18 adds weight to the contention that we should see an allusion to the call of Moses at 2:16.[20]

Paul's sustained comparison of himself and Moses in chapter 3, and the points of commonality that emerge between the two figures, do not, of course, imply that Paul saw himself as a 'second Moses' in line with the expectation of Deuteronomy 18:18. The fulfilment of that role in the New Testament belongs to Jesus alone.[21] Rather, the allusions and references to Moses' ministry serve in a more general way to highlight the fact that, within the context of the new covenant, Paul and his associates' preaching ministry is in some respects equivalent to the prophetic ministry of the Old Testament.

This broader contention is buttressed by the observation that, in addition to establishing this comparison of himself and Moses, Paul aligns his ministry with the prophetic ministry of Isaiah later in the letter. At 6:2 Paul issues God's appeal to his people found in Isaiah 49:8: 'In a favourable time I listened to you, and in a day of salvation I have helped you.' He affirms that 'now', as he issues the divine appeal (5:20; 6:1), is the 'favourable time', 'the day of salvation'. In re-issuing the divine appeal first spoken through Isaiah, Paul indicates that he sees his own ministry as functioning in a way similar to Isaiah's. As was the case in the prophetic ministry of Isaiah, when Paul, God's co-worker, makes God's authoritative appeal to his people, it is indeed the 'favourable time' and 'day of salvation'. As Hafemann notes, '[t]his use of Scripture in 2 Corinthians 6:2, together with its declaration of fulfilment, is one of the strongest assertions of Paul's strategic role within the history of redemption. Paul, like Isaiah, speaks for God, and God speaks through Paul.'[22]

Summary

As Paul reflects on the nature of the preaching ministry he shares with his ministry associates, he attests to a number of characteristics of

---

[20] Thrall (1994: 436), following Bachmann and Wolter, finds a further allusion to the commissioning of Moses at 5:19, where she notes a 'reminiscence of the language of Ps 104 (LXX) 27', which itself 'refers to the commissioning of Moses and Aaron to proclaim to Pharaoh God's message concerning the plagues'. So too Hafemann 2005: 246–247.

[21] So, rightly, Hafemann 2005: 103; see also Aernie 2012: 125–133.

[22] Hafemann 2000b: 249. For further consideration of Paul's self-presentation in the light of Moses and Isaiah in 2 Corinthians, see esp. Hafemann 2005; Aernie 2012: 113–244; and Gignilliat 2007. But note Aernie's (2012: 154–155) judicious evaluation of Gignilliat's thesis.

that ministry and privileges attached to it. The very fact that he presents it as a shared ministry indicates that he does not view the exercise of this ministry as something exclusively tied to his apostolic office. In this ministry, which is fundamentally a public proclamation of Christ grounded in the Scriptures, God the Trinity is at work as the primary agent. Through this new-covenant ministry, which is parallel to the prophetic ministries of Moses and Isaiah in significant respects, the glory of God is revealed and both the preacher and the hearers encounter God. At various points in the discourse Paul's presentation of this ministry indicates that the proclamation had a natural context in the Christian congregation.

Chapter Eight

1 Thessalonians 1 – 2: Preaching the very words of God

In 1 Thessalonians 1 – 2 Paul gives thanks to God for the Thessalonians' reception of and response to his ministry (alongside that of Silas and Timothy). As he does so he illumines his understanding of the nature of their proclamatory activity and of God's attendant activity in the hearts and lives of those who heard. Before turning to observe the text, it will be helpful to recall the summary of Paul and his team's ministry in Thessalonica as recorded in Acts 17:

> Now when they had passed through Amphipolis and Apollonia, they came to Thessalonica, where there was a synagogue of the Jews. And Paul went in, as was his custom, and on three Sabbath days he reasoned with them from the Scriptures, explaining and proving that it was necessary for the Christ to suffer and to rise from the dead, and saying, 'This Jesus, whom I proclaim to you, is the Christ.' And some of them were persuaded and joined Paul and Silas, as did a great many of the devout Greeks and not a few of the leading women. But the Jews were jealous, and taking some wicked men of the rabble, they formed a mob, set the city in an uproar, and attacked the house of Jason, seeking to bring them out to the crowd. And when they could not find them, they dragged Jason and some of the brothers before the city authorities, shouting, 'These men who have turned the world upside down have come here also, and Jason has received them, and they are all acting against the decrees of Caesar, saying that there is another king, Jesus.' And the people and the city authorities were disturbed when they heard these things. And when they had taken money as security from Jason and the rest, they let them go. (Acts 17:1–9)

In light of this important narrative backdrop, we can make a number of observations from Paul's reflections on this time of ministry in 1 Thessalonians 1 – 2.

The ministry Paul recalls is a ministry of authoritative public proclamation

The narrative context of Acts 17 makes it clear that the ministry that Paul undertook in Thessalonica was a ministry of public proclamation. In line with his standard practice, Paul made for the synagogue and preached there over the course of three Sabbath days (Acts 17:1-3). Luke describes his activity in the synagogue in varied terms: 'he *reasoned* with them from the Scriptures, *explaining* and *proving* . . .' (vv. 2–3a; italics mine). As recorded in Luke's account, Paul identified his ministry activity as 'proclamation': 'This Jesus, whom I proclaim [*katangellō*] to you, is the Christ' (v. 3b). The public nature of this proclamation in the synagogue is underlined by the very public reaction it caused, with the city being set in 'an uproar' (v. 5) and the 'city authorities' being called upon (v. 6). This narrative context indicates that the verb *katangellō* carries here the normal semi-technical meaning that we earlier identified: it refers to a public and authoritative act of proclamation made by an authorized agent.

As Paul recalls the visit that he and his associates made to Thessalonica, he refers twice to their 'entry' or 'arrival' (*eisodos*) (1 Thess. 1:9; 2:1) in Thessalonica.[1] The 'arrival' of secular orators in ancient cities was shaped by convention and calculated to attract public attention. Paul's description of their coming to Thessalonica in 2:1–12 was probably designed to show how different their approach was from that of self-aggrandizing secular orators. Although Paul and his associates were fundamentally unlike such orators in many ways, the basis of any comparison with them that Paul intended to make is that, like the secular orators, Paul saw himself and his associates as *public figures* who came to Thessalonica to exercise a *public teaching role*.

Paul describes their public ministry in general terms as 'speaking' or 'declaring' (*lalēsai*) with 'boldness' (2:2), and more specifically as 'proclaiming the gospel of God' (*ekēryxamen*; 2:9). The message came to the believers as something that had been declared and was to be heard, so Paul describes it as a 'word of hearing' (*logon akoēs*; 2:13;

---

[1] The term *eisodos* could speak of either a person's 'entrance'/'arrival', or of the 'reception' he or she received. The former meaning is clearly appropriate to 2:1 and is probably intended at 1:9 as well (as suggested particularly by the fact that the 'report' in 1:9 is 'concerning us', i.e. concerning the missionaries and their arrival, rather than concerning the Thessalonian converts and any response they made). See Green 2002: 105–106; and Winter 1993.

cf. Rom 10:17; Heb. 4:2 and comments *ad loc*). This proclamation carried with it an authoritative charge to respond appropriately: 'we exhorted each one of you and encouraged and charged you to walk in a manner worthy of God, who calls you into his own kingdom and glory' (2:12).

This ministry was a shared ministry

First Thessalonians is signed by 'Paul, Silvanus, and Timothy' (1:1), indicating that those three men are the joint authors, even if Paul took a lead role in its composition.[2] The account in Acts indicates explicitly that Paul and Silas (Silvanus) made the initial journey to Thessalonica (see Acts 16:25; 17:4, 10), but the narrative context suggests that Timothy was probably also with them (Acts 16:3; 17:4). Although the Acts 17 account mentions only Paul's preaching (17:2–3), Paul's own recollections of the ministry in Thessalonica are cast in the first person plural. This use of the plural is most naturally taken as a genuine plural (rather than a merely stylistic 'authorial' plural).[3] Paul's occasional use of the first person singular when he wants to draw attention to his own personal action or viewpoint (2:18; 3:5; 5:27) serves to strengthen the conclusion that the regular use of the plural in 1 Thessalonians represents the joint action of Paul, Silas and Timothy.[4] Thus, even if Paul was the primary preacher in Thessalonica (as we might imagine, given his apostolic status), the recollections of this letter indicate that Silas and Timothy shared in the word ministry during the Thessalonian mission.[5]

The proclamation is made by 'approved' agents

Paul and his companions lay emphasis on the fact that they acted as approved agents in declaring the gospel in Thessalonica:

---

[2] So Green 2002: 82; and Fee 2009: 4.

[3] Fee 2009: 4.

[4] The self-description of the authors as 'apostles of Christ' (2:6) could weigh against the suggestion that the plural is genuine, but here the term 'apostle' does not function as a narrowly technical term for the Twelve. Rather, as Bruce rightly suggests, it 'is used in a rather general sense: Paul associates his companions with his own apostolic ministry – in which indeed they shared' (Bruce 1982b: 31; see also Green 2002: 125–126).

[5] It is important to consider the fact that the Thessalonian mission may have lasted a period of months, and so we should not take the Acts account as a comprehensive record of all the ministry that took place there, but simply as a summary of key events. On the length of the missionaries' stay in Thessalonica see Fee 2009: 6.

For our appeal does not spring from error or impurity or any attempt to deceive, but just as we have been approved by God to be entrusted with the gospel, so we speak, not to please man, but to please God who tests our hearts. For we never came with words of flattery, as you know, nor with a pretext for greed – God is witness. Nor did we seek glory from people, whether from you or from others, though we could have made demands as apostles of Christ. (2:3–6)

The term translated here 'approved' (*dedokimasmetha*) refers to being proved (and ultimately 'approved') through testing. It was used in the ancient world to refer to the testing and approval of office holders for their role.[6] Here the Lord is the one who has tested and proved his agents for work as his gospel ministers (the same verb is used later in 2:4: 'God who tests [*dokimazonti*] our hearts'). Having approved them, the Lord has sent them to speak his word as his 'apostles' (2:6).[7] Silas and Timothy are not part of the Twelve, but they are nonetheless God's authorized agents and, through their association with Paul, they participate in the apostolic ministry. Because these approved agents came speaking God's true word, the word was accepted 'not as the word of men but as what it really is, the word of God' (2:13).[8] Their status as approved agents also carried uncomfortable personal implications for them as speakers. Just as the Old Testament prophets and Jesus himself faced opposition as they proclaimed God's word as his prophetic agents, so too have Paul and his associates faced rejection. Aligning himself, Silas and Timothy with Jesus and the prophets, Paul writes that the Jews 'killed both the Lord Jesus and the prophets, and drove us out' (2:15).[9]

[6] 'In the inscr. Indeed the verb is almost a *term. techn.* for passing as fit for a public office' (MM, p. 167).

[7] Although note that in the Greek text of NA28, the phrase in which this term is found falls in 2:7 not 2:6.

[8] A further point of interest here is the way in which the authenticity of the message is bound up with the character of these authorized agents in 1 Thess. 1 – 2. This is especially striking in 1:5–6, where Paul records that in accepting the message the hearers came also to imitate the messengers: '[O]ur gospel came to you not only in word, but also in power and in the Holy Spirit and with full conviction. You know what kind of men we proved to be among you for your sake. And you became imitators of us and of the Lord, for you received the word in much affliction, with the joy of the Holy Spirit.'

[9] Notice that once again Paul's comments tacitly reflect an affiliation between the ministries of the OT prophets, Jesus and the NT apostles. This point rests on taking the reference to 'prophets' as referring to OT prophets, as seems most natural (cf. Matt. 5:12; 23:29–30), but note Gilliard's (1994) alternative view that the reference is to Christian prophets.

God stands behind this proclamation as the primary actor

Paul and his companions were, of course, the agents of speech and delivery of God's word at Thessalonica. Nevertheless, Paul's discussion of the delivery of that word in 1 Thessalonians betrays the conviction that ultimately God stood behind the proclamation of his word as the primary actor. This belief underpins (and makes sense of) the opening thanksgiving of the letter. Paul writes that they 'give thanks to God always for all of you' (1:2) because 'we know, brothers loved by God, that he has chosen you' (1:4). The evidence of God's election of the Thessalonian believers is that 'our gospel came to you not only in word, but also in power and in the Holy Spirit and with full conviction' (1:5a). That is, because God had chosen the Thessalonian believers, by his Holy Spirit he caused his proclaimed word to come to them with powerful effectiveness, leading them to be convinced of its truth.[10] God brought to fruition his choosing of the Thessalonian believers through the preaching of his word.

The conviction that God spoke through Paul and his associates' preaching is made all the more explicit in 2:12–13. Verse 12 indicates that in their proclamation they acted in parallel with, and as agents of, the God who 'calls' his people: 'we exhorted each one of you and encouraged you and charged you to walk in a manner worthy of God, who calls you into his own kingdom and glory' (2:12). Indeed, their proclamation was nothing less than God's own word: 'And we also thank God constantly for this, that when you received the word of God, which you heard from us, you accepted it not as the word of men, but as what it really is, the word of God' (2:13). 'The preachers were the immediate source of the message. But Paul and his companions were no more than intermediaries in proclaiming a gospel whose ultimate source and originator was none less than God himself.'[11]

---

[10] Fee's (2009: 34–35) analysis here is clear and helpful: '[T]he twin phrases, "but in power" and "with the Holy Spirit and deep conviction", refer primarily to Paul's preaching, but not so much to the *manner* (or style) of the preaching as to its Spirit-empowered *effectiveness* . . . Thus, the Holy Spirit is being designated as the source of the power in his preaching the gospel, the evidence of which was the full conviction that accompanied his preaching and resulted in their conversion' (italics in original).

[11] Morris 1991: 80.

The proclaimed word effects change in the hearers

This final observation follows very naturally from what we have seen so far. In these first two chapters of 1 Thessalonians Paul draws particular attention to the powerful effect that the proclaimed word has had on the lives of the hearers. As a result of the word going out 'in power and in the Holy Spirit and with full conviction' (1:5), the hearers 'became imitators of us and of the Lord' as they 'received the word in much affliction, with the joy of the Holy Spirit' (1:6). Not only has the Holy Spirit empowered the proclamation of the word, but he has also caused the recipients to accept it with conviction of its truth and with joy, even in the context of trial.[12] The result of this Spirit-enabled reception is that the Thessalonians have become an example to others (1:7), having turned from idols to wait for the Son to return (1:9–10). More than that, as a result of hearing and receiving the word, the Thessalonians have themselves become ministers of that word to others (1:8). Paul does not specify the particular manner in which the Thessalonians communicated the word of God to others.[13] Indeed, the word of God itself is the subject of the verb 'sounded forth' [*exērchētai*] at 1:8, emphasizing the fact that it is the word itself which is primarily at work. 'The word is pictured as an active force, radiating out from the Thessalonians by its own power.'[14] Unquestionably, though, Paul attests here to the Thessalonians' participation in mission through actively communicating the word of God.[15]

The effective power of the word to bring about change in the hearers shines through again in Paul's further thanksgiving at 2:13–14. Paul gives thanks that the Thessalonians received the proclaimed word as God's own word, 'which is at work in you believers' (2:13).[16] The

[12] Although the 'conviction' referred to could conceivably point to the conviction with which the messengers spoke the gospel, it is more naturally taken as referring to the conviction with which it was received. 'The reference is to the Thessalonians' deep inward persuasion of the truth of the gospel, a token of the Holy Spirit's work in their hearts' (Bruce 1982b: 14).

[13] Notice that he does *not* say that they 'preached the gospel'. Cf. Ware 1992: 130–131.

[14] Ware 1992: 128.

[15] So Marshall 2000: 259, but *contra* Bowers 1991: 107 and *passim*, who understands Paul simply to refer to the 'common life' of the believers attracting notice. Marshall rightly maintains that the verb 'sounded forth' 'conveys something much more dynamic than a report of somebody's behaviour. It is also curious to describe a report of somebody's conversion as being the content of "the Word of the Lord".'

[16] It is possible that 'God' could be taken as the antecedent of *hos* in 2:13b so that the phrase might be translated '*who* is at work in you believers', but this reading is rendered unlikely by the fact that the verb *energeitai* always has an impersonal subject when used in the middle voice in the NT (Fee 2009: 88). Nonetheless, given the way in

evidence of the activity of the word in them follows immediately: 'For you, brothers, became imitators of the churches of God in Christ Jesus that are in Judea. For you suffered the same things from your own countrymen as they did from the Jews' (2:14). The preached word brings about life change, most clearly demonstrated by a willingness to suffer for the gospel, and leads to further dissemination of the word.

Summary

Again in this letter Paul characterizes preaching as a public proclamation of God's word, evoking a comparative contrast between his band of preachers and secular orators in his description of their arrival and reception in Thessalonica (1:9; 2:1–12). This preaching ministry was shared with Silas and Timothy, and so was not tied exclusively to the apostolic office. At the same time, Paul insists that they were all approved agents for the ministry they undertook (2:4), indicating that preaching is carried out by those with a particular God-given mandate for the task. As we have found in other letters, Paul points to the fact that God is the primary actor standing behind the preaching. Unsurprisingly, God's powerful preached word effects profound change in those who hear and receive it, leading in turn to the further dissemination of the word.

which Paul conceives of God acting by his word, the difference in meaning is slight. Green points out that the verb 'is at work' is used often in the NT 'to talk about God's activity in the human realm' (Green 2002: 140; see also Morris 1991: 81), so even though the 'word' is the subject here, the statement points to God's activity in the lives of the Thessalonians through his word.

Chapter Nine

Hebrews: Preaching to the gathered people of God

Although Hebrews may appear to say little directly on the subject of preaching, it is the one epistle in the New Testament that clearly self-identifies as a sermon, and as such it occupies a unique place in the New Testament in relation to the subject of preaching. Given the unique character and position of Hebrews in this regard, insights we can glean from the discourse about the writer's understanding of the exercise he is engaged in and his expectations for its effects will be particularly significant for our investigation. Hebrews is a relatively lengthy New Testament document, and there is a great deal that we could say, but the following are a few key observations.[17]

Hebrews is a sermon intended to be read aloud in the Christian assembly

Most New Testament epistles have at least some affinity with the sermonic genre in that they were generally designed to be read out to Christian congregations. But Hebrews calls itself a 'word of exhortation' (13:22), which was a term used in contemporary Judaism and early Christianity to refer to the sermon in a synagogue or church gathering. It is used in this way in Acts 13:14–15, where Paul and his companions are invited to preach in the synagogue at Pisidian Antioch: 'After the reading from the Law and the Prophets, the rulers of the synagogue sent a message to them, saying, "Brothers, if you have any word of encouragement [or 'exhortation'] for the people, say it."' Quite clearly, Paul (along with his companions) is being invited to deliver the Sabbath-day sermon.[18] In a later Christian context, a

---

[17] For a more exhaustive treatment of this subject, see Griffiths 2014. The following observations are in large part a summary of some of the findings of that work.

[18] See the similar pattern of Scripture reading followed by preaching in a Christian context suggested by 1 Tim. 4:13: 'Until I come, devote yourself to the public reading of Scripture, to exhortation, to teaching.'

fourth-century liturgy designates the sermon 'words of exhortation' (*Apostolic Constitutions* 8.5).[1]

Added to the designation the writer gives his sermon, the form of the discourse indicates that Hebrews is no ordinary letter. It lacks a traditional epistolary opening, but rather launches straight into the substance of its 'preaching', setting it apart in form from other New Testament letters as more markedly sermonic in genre. A number of features of Hebrews indicate its fundamentally 'oral' rather than written character: the writer's use of the first person plural (which 'enables the speaker to identify with his listeners while addressing them with authority'[2]); frequent references to speaking and hearing, rather than writing (2:5; 6:9; 8:1; 11:32); and the regular alternation between exposition and exhortation.[3] As noted above, Hebrews is arguably the earliest extant full-length Christian sermon.[4]

Hebrews provides a model for us of the shape of Christian preaching

Given that Hebrews occupies this unique place as our earliest record of a complete Christian sermon, it is worth pausing to note the shape and substance of that sermon before proceeding to consider the theological convictions that underlie it. These observations on the level of form and content do not require the conclusion that all Christian sermons must share these characteristics of the Hebrews sermon, but it seems reasonable to assume that there should be valuable lessons here for preachers.

Recent studies of the structure of Hebrews have increasingly recognized the central place of Old Testament texts and themes in the

---

[1] See further discussion in Griffiths 2014: 16–20.

[2] O'Brien 2010: 21.

[3] Johnson 2006: 10; see also Griffiths 2014: 17; O'Brien 2010: 21. It is widely assumed that the sermons recorded in Acts are summaries of longer addresses.

[4] Vanhoye (1989: 3), who has perhaps devoted more attention to the structure and genre of Hebrews than any other recent scholar, concludes that '"The Letter" to the Hebrews is simply not a letter . . . it belongs to the genre of preaching. In fact, it is the only example we have in the New Testament of the text of a sermon which has been preserved in its entirety.' Arguably, the designation 'letter' remains appropriate for Hebrews because the category of 'letter' in the NT is probably broad enough to encompass a written sermon like this one (so, rightly, O'Brien 2010: 21). But Vanhoye's conclusion that Hebrews is fundamentally a sermon is surely correct and is now widely accepted. Cockerill's (2012) recent commentary on Hebrews reflects this conclusion; he regularly refers to the author as the 'pastor' and to the discourse as the 'sermon' (and sometimes also to the intended recipients as the 'congregation').

framing of Hebrews' argument. There is now quite a widespread acknowledgment among commentators and other scholars that Hebrews essentially constitutes a series of expositions of Old Testament texts and themes in light of their fulfilment in Christ. It has been argued elsewhere that each of the structural units of Hebrews (of which there are perhaps eleven) consists of an Old Testament text (or *texts*), an explanation and application of that text to the contemporary congregation in light of Christ, and then an exhortation to respond appropriately (hence the frequent refrain, 'Therefore, let us . . .').[5]

Identification of this repeated structural pattern highlights two key features of the Hebrews sermon that modern preachers would surely do well to emulate. First, it is fundamentally an exposition of Scripture in light of Christ. Second, exegesis and doctrinal teaching always lead to heart-engaging, urgent exhortation.

'Speaking the word' through preaching is a characteristic function of the post-apostolic leaders of the church

Hebrews was written by an unnamed Christian leader who, with the church he addresses, was brought to faith through the eyewitness testimony of those who heard Jesus (presumably, but not necessarily, apostles; 2:3–4). He does not suggest that he was an eyewitness or apostle himself. Although he is not present with the congregation he addresses (he longs to be restored to them soon, 13:19), he indicates that he views himself as a leader of the congregation and sends his sermon to them in the capacity of a leader.

In the final chapter of Hebrews the writer instructs the congregation concerning the nature of 'acceptable worship' of God (a theme introduced at 12:28–29). Within this section on worship, the writer devotes considerable attention to the attitude of the people towards their leaders, with this theme dominating 13:7–24. It will be helpful to trace the flow of logic here. He begins by urging the people (as an act of 'acceptable worship'), 'Remember your leaders, those who spoke to you the word of God' (13:7). These former leaders, who are presumably now dead, are to be remembered primarily as those who spoke the word of God to the people. Next, he tells the congregation, 'Obey your [current] leaders and submit to them, for they are keeping watch

---

[5] See Griffiths 2014: 28, 35.

over your souls, as those who will have to give an account' (13:17a). The writer then proceeds in the next verse to ask for prayer for himself (by implication grouping himself with the leaders mentioned in the previous verse): 'Pray for us, for we are sure that we have a clear conscience, desiring to act honourably in all things' (13:18).[6] The writer asks for prayer for himself as a leader who will have to give account for his leadership within the congregation. He testifies that he has a clear conscience, presumably at least in part because he has 'kept watch' over the souls of the congregation before him by speaking faithfully the word of God to them, that they might submit to it (see 13:17). He has done this not least through the sermon he is writing to them. And so he asks them to bear with this 'word of exhortation' (13:22) – that they might receive and submit to the word, and benefit from doing so.

In a context where there does not appear to be current apostolic leadership within the congregation, it is striking to note that leaders are established to whom the people of God must submit. The necessity of submission to these leaders is presumably not simply due to their position or office. These leaders, like those who went before (13:7) and like the writer of Hebrews (13:22), are undoubtedly those who speak the word of God to the people of God. Submission to them, then, is submission to the word of God as it is spoken.

In placing himself and his leadership alongside that of the other contemporary leaders of the congregation, the writer of Hebrews sets his preaching (specifically, the preaching recorded in his 'word of exhortation') alongside their preaching. Despite the fact that, under the sovereignty of God, the preaching of this particular leader is also inspired Scripture (and therefore its content stands apart from other Christian preaching in its normative and abiding authority), this observation indicates to us that the writer sees his preaching as also occupying a normal place within the life of a post-apostolic congregation. The Hebrews sermon constitutes an authoritative declaration of the word of God by a post-apostolic leader of the congregation. Thus, in some significant respects, it stands in a position partially parallel to (but clearly not identical with) contemporary preaching today.

---

[6] The first person plural here may be an authorial plural meaning 'me', or it may be a genuine plural, in which case the writer is speaking as one leader of the congregation on behalf of all the leaders.

The writer believes that in his sermon he is speaking God's word

Hebrews has a robust theology of the word of God. It opens by addressing the question of how God speaks (1:1–4), and it contains one of the most direct and substantial statements in the New Testament concerning the power of the word: 'For the word of God [*ho logos tou theou*] is living and active, sharper than any two-edged sword, piercing to the division of soul and of spirit, of joints and of marrow, and discerning the thoughts and intentions of the heart' (4:12). The theology of the word is a central theme and concern of the discourse, and the writer makes use of the term 'the word' [*ho logos*] with a high degree of consistency throughout his sermon to refer to a divine message with its origin in God; that is, he typically uses the term to refer to *God's word*.

The term 'the word' [*ho logos*; with the article] appears at 2:2; 4:2, 12, 13; 5:11, 13; 6:1; 7:28; 13:7, 22. It is immediately clear in most of these cases that the 'word' or message referred to is a form of God's word: 'the word declared by angels' (that is, the covenant at Sinai, 2:2); 'the message [*ho logos*] they [the wilderness generation] heard' (4:2); 'the word of God' (4:12, already noted); 'the word of righteousness' (probably the gospel message that establishes positional righteousness and encourages righteous living, 5:13); 'the word of Christ' (probably the basic gospel message, 6:1); 'the word of the oath' (7:28; God's oath of Ps. 110:4, fulfilled in Christ); and 'the word of God' spoken by former leaders (13:7).[7]

Given that the writer regularly uses the term 'the word' to refer to a word or message that comes from God, it is significant to note that on a number of occasions he designates the word spoken or preached by the leaders of God's people as 'the word' [*ho logos*]. He says that former leaders of the congregation 'spoke the word of God' (*ton logon tou theou*, 13:7) to the church addressed in Hebrews.[8] He then asks the congregation to bear with the 'word of exhortation' (*tou logou tēs paraklēseōs*, 13:22) that he is presently bringing them.

On two previous occasions (arguably at 4:13, quite clearly at 5:11) he has similarly referred to his own sermon as 'the word'. At 4:13,

---

[7] O'Brien (2010: 175) similarly notes of the writer's use of *logos* (with specific reference to Heb. 2:2; 4:2; 5:13; 6:1; 7:28; 12:19; and 13:7) that '[i]n each instance, *logos* refers to a speech or reality that takes its origin in God'.

[8] Note the use of the extended phrase 'the word of God' here, as used also in the key statement in 4:12.

translators usually render the Greek phrase *pros hon hēmin ho logos* by the translation 'to whom we must give account' (or a close English equivalent). They do so based on the assumption that the writer here makes use of an idiom borrowed from the commercial sphere ('to render account'). However, based upon the pattern of lexical and syntactical features typically present when that idiom is used elsewhere in the New Testament, it seems quite unlikely that the writer adopts that idiom here.[9] It seems much more likely that (in parallel with 5:11) the phrase means 'concerning whom is my word' – or, more fluidly rendered, 'about whom I am speaking'.[10] If this is correct, then the term *ho logos* refers to the writer's discourse here at 4:13. Similarly, at 5:11 the writer refers to his sermon as 'the word' (*ho logos*), using a similar construction: *Peri hou polys hēmin ho logos* ('About this we have much to say').[11] Given that the writer has used the term 'the word' with a high degree of consistency elsewhere to refer unambiguously to God's own 'word', his use of the term 'the word' to refer to his sermon on three occasions (4:13; 5:11; and 13:22) is suggestive of a high theological view of the nature of his discourse.[12]

Such an impression is reinforced at various stages throughout the sermon. In chapters 3 and 4, the writer repeatedly draws the congregation's attention to the appeal of Psalm 95:7–8, 'Today, if you hear his voice, do not harden your hearts . . .' We are naturally prompted to ask how it is that the people might hear God's voice 'today'. It takes only a moment's reflection to realize that, in the first instance, it is as the writer expounds God's word through his own sermon that the

---

[9] Smillie (2005) observes that on each occasion when that idiom is used elsewhere in the NT (as it is in Heb. 13:17), certain features are normally present, all of which are absent here: the term *logos* is used without the article and is in the accusative case, functioning as the object of the verb *apodidōmi* or *didōmi*. See also discussion in Griffiths 2014: 84–88.

[10] This suggestion makes good contextual sense in the light of the immediate move to a consideration of Christ the High Priest in the following verse (which would otherwise seem to be a rather unnatural shift). Taking into account the proposed emendation, Heb. 4:13–14 would read: 'And no creature is hidden from his sight, but all are naked and exposed to the eyes of him about whom I am speaking. Since then we have a great high priest who has passed through the heavens, Jesus, the Son of God . . .'

[11] The writer's use of the dative of possession ('to us'; rather than the genitive, which we might sooner expect) in both these instances may point to the fact that his message is something that he has received from the Lord.

[12] Indeed, if it is accepted that the writer views his own sermon as a form of God's 'word', then every use of the term *logos* in Hebrews refers to a form of God's word, except at 13:17 (where the term serves as part of the commercial idiom 'render account').

congregation will hear God's voice. The poignancy of the refrain from Psalm 95 derives from the fact that the people gathered to listen to the Hebrews sermon are that very moment hearing God's voice 'today'.

In quite a similar way, the writer exhorts the congregation, 'See that you do not refuse him who is speaking. For if they did not escape when they refused him who warned them on earth, much less will we escape if we reject him who warns from heaven' (12:25). This speaker who must not be refused is not explicitly named here. The wider context makes it clear that, in an ultimate sense, the speaker must be God himself (the one whose voice shakes the earth, 12:26). However, in an immediate sense, the voice the congregation are hearing as they listen to the sermon is the preacher's voice. He is, if you like, the mouthpiece of God for them, and they are called to respond rightly to God's word as the preacher declares it. Thus the ambiguity of the identity of the speaker at 12:25 is perhaps no accident on the part of the writer. The congregation are not to reject the 'one who is speaking', because the living God is speaking through the person who is standing before them speaking on his behalf. Like the preachers of former days (13:7), the writer of Hebrews sees himself as one who 'speaks the word of God' to the people.

The preaching act carries judicial implications and offers the opportunity to access the place of divine rest

Here we are particularly concerned with Hebrews 3 – 4. The writer exhorts the congregation to hold fast to their hope in Christ and their confession of him (3:6), and he frames his appeal using the words of Psalm 95:7–8 (Heb. 3:7–8). We suggested above that the voice of God is heard in and through the delivery of the Hebrews sermon as Scripture is expounded. Having heard the voice of God, the people are to exhort one another daily to continue to respond rightly to it (3:13). The writer then reminds the people that a former generation (the wilderness generation of whom Ps. 95 speaks) heard God's voice but rebelled against him (3:16), and so were denied entry to the land of promise (3:17–19). The contemporary believers and the wilderness generation stand in significantly parallel situations: 'For good news came to us [euēngelismenoi] just as to them, but the message they heard [ho logos tēs akoēs] did not benefit them, because they were not united by faith with those who listened' (4:2).

The former delivery of good news that the writer has in mind seems to be the announcement made by Joshua and Caleb to the congregation in the wilderness concerning the goodness of the promised land and the fact that the Lord would give it to his people, in keeping with his promise:[13]

Then Moses and Aaron fell on their faces before all the assembly of the congregation of the people of Israel. And Joshua the son of Nun and Caleb the son of Jephunneh, who were among those who had spied out the land, tore their clothes and said to all the congregation of the people of Israel, 'The land, which we passed through to spy it out, is an exceedingly good land. If the LORD delights in us, he will bring us into this land and give it to us, a land that flows with milk and honey. Only do not rebel against the LORD. And do not fear the people of the land, for they are bread for us. Their protection is removed from them, and the LORD is with us; do not fear them.' Then all the congregation said to stone them with stones. But the glory of the LORD appeared at the tent of meeting to all the people of Israel. (Num. 14:5–10)

To the writer of Hebrews, that announcement of the goodness of the land and of God's intention and ability to deliver the land into their hands was an announcement of 'good news'. It was essentially a re-affirmation of the covenant promises to Israel. However, as Numbers dramatically recounts and Hebrews notes, the people rebelled and did not listen and respond with faith to the announcement of good news.

The writer refers to this announcement of good news using the verb *euangelizomai*. The context here in 4:2 shows that the communication in view is a public announcement of good news, grounded in Scripture, to the congregation of God's people. This indicates that the verb once again bears its semi-technical meaning, signifying a public proclamation, or preaching, of the good news. That conclusion is further supported by the use of the term 'word of hearing' (*logos tēs akoēs*) to describe the message. As we found in the exegesis of Romans 10, the term 'hearing' (*akoē*) can refer to a message that is proclaimed (and so heard). Such is the case in LXX Isaiah 52:7 and 53:1, and Paul

---

[13] This suggestion not only fits with the clear reference here in the immediate context back to the wilderness generation and its rebellion, but it also resonates with a broader observation about this section of Hebrews: namely, that much of Heb. 3 – 5 follows and expounds the narrative of Num. 12 – 16. For further discussion of this point see Griffiths 2014: 33–34.

follows that use in Romans 10:16 (see also Gal. 3:2, 5; 1 Thess. 2:13).[14] The matching of the term 'hearing' here with the term 'word of' suggests that the emphasis falls on the character of the message rather than on its means of reception, so the phrase 'word of hearing' means the 'preached' or 'declared' word.[15]

For the wilderness generation, the proclaimed good news (and their subsequent response to it) was the key to their entry to the promised land. As a whole congregation, they disbelieved the word, rebelled, and so were refused entry. The writer points out that, in a parallel way, he and the congregation he addresses have heard a proclaimed message of good news themselves – presumably here referring back to their own conversion through the testimony of eyewitnesses of Jesus (Heb. 2:3–4). And so for them, their response (both initial and continuing) to the preached word is essential for entry to the divine rest, which is now no longer the land, but rather God's eternal rest in his presence (4:3–10).

The writer establishes the fact that God's rest remains available, and he reminds the people that if they should hear God's voice 'today', they must respond rightly (4:6–7). The 'today' of hearing God's voice is contemporized as the people listen to the sermon. As the congregation of God's people hear God's word the opportunity of entering his promised rest is reaffirmed and the call to respond is issued afresh. Nevertheless, as was the case for the wilderness generation, the congregation must recognize that the 'word of God' which they are hearing preached to them is not simply for their comfort, but can also be for their judgment (4:11–13). If God's people respond in faith to the preached word, they will enter God's rest. If they respond in unbelieving rebellion, they will be judged and excluded. Such are the stakes when the gospel is preached. They were the stakes in the wilderness; they were the stakes when the Hebrews congregation was first evangelized; and the writer makes it clear that they remain so as he delivers his word to them.

The writer expects the congregation to encounter Christ as he preaches the word

This suggestion flows from three related features of Hebrews: first, its general theology of the word; second, its regular invitations to

---

[14] See further discussion in Griffiths 2014: 70–73.

[15] Note also that in Isa. 53:1 the term *akoē* (with the meaning 'message') is used in conjunction with the verb *euangelizomai*, as here in Heb. 4:2.

'approach' God; and, third, its portrayal of the heavenly Zion in chapter 12. We will consider each briefly in turn.

The writer's theology of the word

The writer makes it clear at the opening of his discourse that the Son of God is the supreme expression of the word of God. God has revealed himself through all that the Son is and has done. Verses 1 to 4 of Hebrews 1 constitute one extended sentence in the original, and express together the way in which God has spoken by (or, more literally, '*in*') his Son:

> Long ago, at many times and in many ways, God spoke to our fathers by the prophets, but in these last days he has spoken to us by his Son, whom he appointed the heir of all things, through whom also he created the world. He is the radiance of the glory of God and the exact imprint of his nature, and he upholds the universe by the word of his power. After making purification for sins, he sat down at the right hand of the Majesty on high, having become as much superior to angels as the name he has inherited is more excellent than theirs.

This supreme revelation of God in the Son is both final and personal. It is final because it comes at the last stage of salvation history ('in these last days') and because it is complete, unlike the comparatively piecemeal ('at many times and in many ways') revelation of God in former times. The words of the prophets pointed forward to the Son and his work, and it follows that everything spoken after the incarnation, life, death, resurrection and ascension of the Son (including the writer's sermon) simply re-expresses and expounds this supreme and final revelation of God in the Son.

The revelation of God in the Son is personal in that it is expressed not merely in propositions that the Son makes, but in all that he does and says (as outlined in vv. 2–4). It might seem remarkable that Hebrews, which opens with this majestic statement concerning the revelation of God in the Son, never explicitly quotes from the teaching ministry of Jesus. Instead the writer concerns himself throughout the letter with expounding the significance of Jesus' Person and work. Like the Prologue of John's Gospel, Hebrews 1 shows evidence of a 'word Christology', where the word of God finds supreme expression in the Person of Christ. This theological understanding becomes evident at other points in the letter, notably at Hebrews 12:24, where we are told

113

that the 'sprinkled blood' of Jesus 'speaks' from Zion.[16] It similarly shines through in the fascinating statement in 2:9 that at the present time 'we see him' (that is, Christ). Only a few verses earlier the writer has made it clear that he and the congregation were not primary eye-witnesses of the ministry of Jesus (2:3) – and in any case, he is writing after the time of the ascension. Nonetheless, he and his congregation 'see' Jesus. How is this happening? The primary activity the writer is engaged in is 'speaking' (2:5), and the subject of his speaking is an exposition of Psalm 8 and Christ's exaltation in the world to come, in fulfilment of that psalm. Hebrews has already made it clear that the word of God is supremely expressed in the Person of Christ. Thus to speak his word (in expounding his written, scriptural word) or to read his word written is to encounter Christ and to hear him speak. For the writer, this surely takes place in any context where the word is opened – and not least in and through preaching as he 'speaks' the word.

The repeated invitation to 'approach' God

Given what we have said so far, it should come as little surprise that as the writer expounds the written word in light of its fulfilment in Christ the great High Priest, his natural inclination is to call the people of God to approach God through Christ. The writer never stops at simply speaking about Christ; he proclaims Christ from the Scriptures, and then exhorts believers to come near to him. Having warned the people of the reality of judgment as they hear the word preached, at the end of chapter 4 the writer issues an invitation (grounded in deep reassurance) to come near to Christ:

> Since then we have a great high priest who has passed through the heavens, Jesus, the Son of God, let us hold fast our confession. For we do not have a high priest who is unable to sympathize with our weaknesses, but one who in every respect has been tempted as we are, yet without sin. Let us then with confidence draw near to the throne of grace, that we may receive mercy and find grace to help in time of need. (4:14–16)

[16] Heb. 6:17 is another fascinating instance where God's word is expressed through the Person and work of the Son. This is obscured in English translations, but there the writer affirms that God 'mediated [*emesiteusen*] his purpose with an oath' (tr. mine). Jesus is presented as the supreme mediator between God and his people in Hebrews (and is named the 'mediator' [*mesitēs*] at 8:6; 9:15; and 12:24), and the oath of God (here referring to the oath of Ps. 110:4) is fulfilled in the personal mediation of Christ the High Priest of his people. For a full discussion of this point, see Griffiths 2014: 106, 125.

Similarly, in chapter 10, after a long exposition concerning Jesus' high priesthood, the writer calls the congregation to come near to the One he has proclaimed:

> Therefore, brothers, since we have confidence to enter the holy places by the blood of Jesus, by the new and living way that he opened for us through the curtain, that is, through his flesh, and since we have a great priest over the house of God, let us draw near with a true heart in full assurance of faith, with our hearts sprinkled clean from an evil conscience and our bodies washed with pure water. Let us hold fast the confession of our hope without wavering, for he who promised is faithful. And let us consider how to stir up one another to love and good works, not neglecting to meet together, as is the habit of some, but encouraging one another, and all the more as you see the Day drawing near. (10:19–25)

This repeated call and invitation gains added significance as we remember the initial intended context for the Hebrews sermon: it was designed to be read out to the gathered people of God – hence the corporate significance of the call to consider how to encourage 'one another' and the injunction to keep on meeting together. The writer has in mind the assembly in the first instance. Moreover, the language of 'approach' and 'drawing near' used in these passages in Hebrews [the key verb is *proserchomai*] is borrowed from the world of temple worship. The priests 'approached' God in the sanctuary under the old covenant; but now the whole people of God can approach God through Christ their priest. However, the democratization of this divine approach under the new covenant does not make it a purely personal matter. No doubt the writer intends the people to understand that they can approach God through Christ at any time and in any place; but the initial context of the appeal is to approach *together*, within the setting of corporate worship, in response to the proclamation of Christ from his word. The Jesus who is present by his word and who is seen as his word is proclaimed is truly among his people and invites them to come near to him by faith.

The portrayal of the heavenly Zion in Hebrews 12

In Hebrews 12:22–24, the writer draws the eyes of the congregation to look by faith at the heavenly destination to which they have come in Christ:

> But you have come to Mount Zion and to the city of the living God, the heavenly Jerusalem, and to innumerable angels in festal gathering, and to the assembly of the firstborn who are enrolled in heaven, and to God, the judge of all, and to the spirits of the righteous made perfect, and to Jesus, the mediator of a new covenant, and to the sprinkled blood that speaks a better word than the blood of Abel.

When the writer declares that 'you have come' (*proselēlythate*; perfect tense), he points back to the conversion of the people he addresses. In coming to Christ by faith, they have become citizens of the heavenly city, and so the writer is reaffirming something that has already happened, rather than suggesting that anything new is taking place as he preaches to them. However, as he paints a picture of this city, which is as yet unseen, he points especially to its character as a place where God's people (and his angels) *gather* in his presence. Here are 'innumerable angels in festal gathering' and the 'assembly' (the *ekklēsia*, that is, 'church' or 'congregation') of 'the firstborn who are enrolled in heaven'. Having come by faith, the believers addressed in Hebrews are already enrolled in heaven and are already 'there', on one level, through their union with Christ (see also Eph. 2:6). But there is a special significance to this imagery for a gathering of God's people who are together meeting with Christ by his word. There is a sense in which the gathering addressed by Hebrews is a microcosm and a visible manifestation on earth of the heavenly assembly of all God's people. As the people of God gather to hear his word, they point in a special way to the reality pictured.[17]

For the writer, the sense that this congregation on earth is experiencing something of the heavenly reality of meeting in Christ's presence is heightened by the reminder that they are hearing the 'sprinkled blood' of Christ that 'speaks' (presumably as they listen to the gospel being preached, 12:24). More than that, they are hearing God himself addressing them from heaven (12:25). Again, this speech is heard through the exposition and declaration of his word by the preacher. As the writer expounds Scripture and declares it to the gathered people of God, they are drawn (albeit in a limited and partial way) into the reality of the heavenly gathering in God's

---

[17] Cockerill makes a similar point in his comment on 12:23: 'In their present worship they [the congregation hearing the Hebrews sermon] echo his praise and exult in his triumph. The hearers join all the faithful, past and present, living and dead, in the presence of God on the heavenly Mount Zion' (Cockerill 2012: 655).

presence and they experience proleptically a measure of what they will experience in full in the age to come.

Summary

As the only full-length sermon recorded in the New Testament, Hebrews gives us special insight into the nature of early Christian preaching and its theological character according to Scripture. By its shape and character the Hebrews sermon highlights the fact that preaching (at least for this NT writer) consisted fundamentally in proclaiming Christ through the exposition of Scripture and exhorting hearers to respond. The writer clearly believes that his proclamation of Christ from Scripture is rightly viewed as a 'word' from God (4:13; 5:11; 13:22). We might think that such a high view of the discourse rightly pertains only to this writer, given that his discourse was accepted within the canon of New Testament Scripture. He, however, views the function of 'speaking the word of God' as something that is characteristic of church leaders generally, rather than of him uniquely (13:7).

For the writer of Hebrews, the word of God is supremely expressed in the person of the Son, so it is no surprise that he moves seamlessly from proclaiming the word of God to inviting his hearers to approach the presence of God through Christ. There is a real sense that the proclamation of the word of God facilitates a personal encounter with God. When preaching is set in this light, it is natural that the writer should present his preaching as an event carrying judicial implications. As hearers of God's word encounter God (who is both Judge and Saviour) through his word, they must respond rightly in faith or face the danger of losing out on salvation. At the same time, however, this proclaimed word offers access to the heavenly rest of God. The context in view for the Hebrews sermon is the gathering of God's people. This point is not merely a matter of practicality, nor is it theologically incidental; rather, the proclamation of the word of God to the assembly of God's people is the special means by which God's people hear God address them from heaven. And as the gathered people of God listen to God's word in scattered locations throughout the world, they mirror – in a limited but profound way – the heavenly assembly of which they are a part.

Part III:
Summary and conclusions

Chapter Ten

Summary and conclusions

This final section of the study naturally falls into two parts: first, a summary of key exegetical findings; and, second, a consideration of some of the broader implications of these findings for our understanding of the nature of preaching according to the New Testament, especially in the light of biblical theology.

Summary of exegetical findings

1. While a range of Greek vocabulary is used to designate the activity of communicating God's word, the verbs *euangelizomai*, *katangellō* and *kēryssō* are used with a high degree of consistency throughout the New Testament to denote the public, authoritative declaration of God's word by a commissioned leader. These verbs are rightly classified as 'semi-technical' terms meaning 'to preach' and regularly function as near equivalents. Further, of these three semi-technical terms, *kēryssō* is used with the highest degree of consistency in the New Testament to bear this meaning and has the narrowest semantic range, centred on the meaning 'to preach'.

2. There is ground for speaking of a formally identifiable activity in the New Testament called 'preaching' which is distinguishable from other forms of word ministry, although closely related to them. Observation of this phenomenon (and instructions related to it) in the New Testament points to the following characteristics as defining it in relation to other forms of word ministry:
    (a) It is a proclamation of God's word, and especially the gospel of Jesus Christ;
    (b) It is carried out by recognized leaders with a commission to preach;
    (c) It is an authoritative proclamation;
    (d) It is carried out in a public context.

3. The New Testament presents Jesus, the apostles, their agents and other unidentified church leaders as preachers. It indicates that their preaching stands in a line of continuity with prophetic

ministry in the Old Testament, and it further demonstrates an expectation that preaching will continue beyond the apostolic age.

4. On a number of occasions (including Rom. 10; 2 Cor. 3; 1 Thess. 1 – 2; Heb. 4 and 12), the New Testament presents God as speaking through preaching, standing behind the proclamation of his word as the primary actor.

5. On a number of occasions (in 2 Cor. 3 and repeatedly in Hebrews), the New Testament indicates that preaching leads to an encounter with God through Christ.

6. The New Testament regularly reflects the expectation that God's people should respond to the preaching of the word of God in faith and obedience.

7. Hebrews (especially chs. 3 – 4 and 12) and 2 Corinthians (especially ch. 3) reflect the expectation that preaching should take place within the context of the Christian assembly.

Biblical-theological conclusions

As we draw together these exegetical findings and consider their implications within the context of the whole of Scripture and some broad outlines of biblical theology, a number of conclusions concerning the nature of preaching according to the New Testament emerge:

Preaching is a proclamation of the word of God

Across the New Testament evidence surveyed in this study, it has been evident that the substance of preaching is consistently the Person and work of Christ from Scripture. Although Jesus and the apostles were not always explicitly expounding a biblical text in their preaching (even if they were frequently doing so), their proclamation was always of Christ as the one who fulfils the institutions and promises of the Old Testament. Moving beyond the preaching of Jesus and the apostles into the post-apostolic context, it becomes all the more clear that Christian preaching proclaims Christ from Scripture, in accordance with the apostolic teaching. Timothy's charge is to 'preach the word' (2 Tim. 4:2). The context makes it clear that this 'word' is the scriptural word that speaks of salvation through Christ (2 Tim. 3:15–17). For Paul and his ministry associates in Corinth, new-covenant ministry is fundamentally a proclamation of Christ from the Scriptures (1 Cor. 1:17; 2:2; 15:3–5), now with the 'veil' removed (2 Cor. 3:14–16). The Hebrews sermon as a whole is firmly grounded in the exposition of Scripture in light of Christ.

However, the New Testament indicates that the relationship between God's word and faithful preaching is more integral than simply affirming that God's word must be the *content* of Christian preaching. It is not merely that preachers point their hearers' attention to the written word of God and so to Christ, the personal Word of God. (Indeed, if that were the sum total of the preaching task, we might have expected Paul to charge Timothy simply to 'read the word' rather than 'preach it'.) The New Testament makes it clear that preachers act as God's heralds who proclaim his word on his behalf. When authentic, faithful Christian preaching of the biblical word takes place, *that preaching constitutes a true proclamation of the word of God that enables God's own voice to be heard.* This is the implication of Paul's teaching concerning the commissioning of preachers in Romans 10; it is the force of Timothy's commission in 2 Timothy 4:2; it is the plain implication of 1 Thessalonians 2:13; and it is manifestly the conviction of the writer of Hebrews, who believes that through his preached 'word' the living God is addressing his people 'today'.

Christian preaching stands in a line of continuity with the preaching of Jesus and the apostles

A key question for this investigation has been whether or not the New Testament establishes a real link between the preaching of Jesus, the apostles and their agents (like Timothy and Titus) and preaching today. It is one thing to say that *they* had a mandate to preach God's word. It is encouraging to see how the Holy Spirit was clearly at work through *their* preaching. But should their model of preaching shed any light on what preachers do in our day? Do any Christians today have a mandate to do the kind of thing they did in their day?

Various observations and findings from this study have pointed to substantial lines of continuity from the preaching of Jesus to that of the apostles and post-apostolic preachers. At this juncture it will be helpful to draw together those observations, to supplement them with brief reference to a few other key New Testament texts, and to trace that line of continuity.

The work of preaching is given special dignity by the fact that Jesus identified his role in his earthly ministry as primarily that of a preacher. A range of passages throughout the Synoptic Gospels highlight this priority. Mark records Jesus speaking to his disciples at the opening of his ministry, saying, 'Let us go on to the next towns, that I may preach [*kēryxō*] there also, for that is what I came for' (Mark 1:38).

At the opening of his ministry in Luke's account, Jesus enters the synagogue at Nazareth and reads from Isaiah 61:1–2:

> The Spirit of the Lord is upon me,
>   because he has anointed me
>   to proclaim good news [*euangelisasthai*] to the poor.
> He has sent me to proclaim [*kēryxai*] liberty to the captives
>   and recovering of sight to the blind,
>   to set at liberty those who are oppressed,
> to proclaim [*kēryxai*] the year of the Lord's favour.
>
> (Luke 4:18–19)

Jesus identifies himself as the one who fulfils the role of the anointed messenger of Isaiah 61, proclaiming 'good news' (Luke 4:21). In Matthew 9 Jesus is shown to be at work doing what he said he would do at the outset of his ministry – preaching the gospel:

> And Jesus went throughout all the cities and villages, teaching in their synagogues and proclaiming [or 'preaching'; *kēryssōn*] the gospel of the kingdom and healing every disease and every affliction. When he saw the crowds, he had compassion for them, because they were harassed and helpless, like sheep without a shepherd. Then he said to his disciples, 'The harvest is plentiful, but the labourers are few; therefore pray earnestly to the Lord of the harvest to send out labourers into his harvest. (Matt. 9:35–38)

Jesus then proceeds almost immediately to provide an initial answer to his own prayer. He calls his twelve disciples to him, gives them authority over evil spirits and diseases (10:1) and sends them out on mission (from this point on the 'disciples' start to be called 'apostles'):

> These twelve Jesus sent out, instructing them, 'Go nowhere among the Gentiles and enter no town of the Samaritans, but go rather to the lost sheep of the house of Israel. And proclaim [or 'preach'; *kēryssete*] as you go, saying, "The kingdom of heaven is at hand."' (Matt. 10:5–7)

The apostles are given the same message to preach that Jesus preached at the opening of his ministry (and presumably throughout it too; see Matt. 4:17). As apostles, they are to perform miracles that will confirm the truth of their message (we see this throughout the early proclamation of the gospel in the Gospels and Acts), and they are to pronounce judgment on those places that do not respond to the preached word. In short, the apostles will go out and do what Jesus does and speak what he speaks to increase the reach of his ministry – a mandate that flows from Jesus' compassionate concern for the crowds of people he sees before him. Strikingly, Jesus goes on to insist that the apostles are to be treated as his true agents. Indeed, the people's response to them constitutes a response to him: 'Whoever receives you receives me, and whoever receives me receives him who sent me' (Matt. 10:40). The apostles (including, crucially, the latecomer Paul; see Gal. 1:11–17) have a commission to carry on the preaching ministry of Jesus as true and authoritative representatives of Jesus. Their preaching stands in a line of continuity with his.

A number of key New Testament passages that we have considered trace this line of continuity forward from the apostles. In Ephesians 4 Paul reminds us that in his ascension, Jesus gave gifts to his people for the good of the church (4:7–10). In particular, he appointed people to particular roles 'to equip the saints for the work of ministry, for building up the body of Christ' (4:12): 'And he gave the apostles, the prophets, the evangelists, the shepherds and teachers' (4:11). The apostles were to be authoritative teachers and leaders of the church to establish correct doctrine, while the 'prophets' referred to here (as elsewhere in Ephesians; see 2:20; 3:5) occupy a foundational role in teaching doctrine and, quite probably, participating in writing elements of the New Testament.[1] The roles envisaged in the reference to 'the evangelists, the shepherds and teachers' in Ephesians 4:11 are of 'ministers' within the church, and O'Brien rightly affirms that '[w]e may assume that . . . their ministries were accepted and recognized in the churches. It is appropriate, then, to speak of them as "officers".'[2]

In 2 Timothy 1:11 Paul describes himself as a 'preacher and apostle and teacher'. At the end of his life and apostolic ministry he charges Timothy to carry on the work of preaching himself (4:2; cf. 1:13) and, more than that, to train others to carry on the work of word ministry: '[W]hat you have heard from me in the presence of many witnesses entrust to faithful men who will be able to teach others also' (2:2). It seems right to conclude that the 'evangelists', 'shepherds' and 'teachers' Paul refers to in Ephesians 4:11 are the kind of 'faithful men' to whom

---

[1] On the foundational role of these 'prophets', see extended discussions in O'Brien 1999: 214–216, 231–234 and 298.

[2] O'Brien 1999: 301. The status of these figures as recognized office holders is strongly implied by their grouping alongside the 'apostles' and 'prophets'.

Timothy is to entrust the gospel deposit and who will carry on the ministry of preaching the word beyond Timothy's day (note that the charge to 'preach the word' in 2 Tim. 4:2 includes the instruction to 'do the work of an evangelist', 4:5).

In 2 Timothy Paul establishes a clear line of continuity between his apostolic preaching ministry and the preaching ministry of Timothy, and he indicates that Timothy should prioritize training others who will follow after him, who will in turn train others who will follow them. Paul stops short of saying explicitly in 2:2 that Timothy's ministry trainees should 'preach', but it seems reasonable to assume that Paul expected that they would engage in the same kinds of ministries that he and Timothy engaged in, including preaching. So 2 Timothy gives evidence that the activity of preaching is not restricted to the apostolic office, but continues beyond it.

Romans 10 similarly shows that Paul expected the ministry of preaching to continue beyond his day. The preaching of the gospel is the centrepiece of God's plan for salvation for Jew and Gentile, and as Paul asks, 'how are they to hear without someone preaching?' (Rom. 10:14). Elsewhere in Paul's letters this same expectation of the continuation of preaching beyond the apostolic day is reflected implicitly through Paul's description of his preaching activity as one that is shared with his associates. We have seen that it is sometimes a challenge to specify Paul's intent when he uses the first person plural in his letters. However, in 2 Corinthians 1:19 Paul specifies that his reflections on the preaching ministry exercised at Corinth (in that section of the letter, at least) refer to a shared ministry: 'For the Son of God, Jesus Christ, whom we proclaimed among you, Silvanus and Timothy and I . . .'

These combined observations establish the conclusion that the preaching ministry of Jesus and his apostles provides the model and theological basis for the preaching ministries church leaders exercise today. Although preachers today are not in the positions of unique authority of Jesus or his apostles (or of the foundational NT 'prophets'), it is nonetheless valid – indeed necessary – to draw lessons about preaching from what we observe in the New Testament of their preaching ministries.

Christian preaching stands in a line of continuity with the Old Testament prophetic tradition

Post-apostolic preaching ministry not only stands in a line of continuity with the ministry of Jesus, his apostles and their agents, but, together with those ministries, also stands in a line of continuity with prophetic ministry in the Old Testament. Ever since the ministry of Moses, who is the archetypal Old Testament prophet, there has been the promise of a prophet like him being raised up (Deut. 18:15). All Old Testament prophets stood in a line of continuity with this promise and in partial fulfilment of it, but Jesus is the true and ultimate fulfilment of that promise (see John 1:14–18 and Heb. 1:1–4). There is no new revelation concerning God's identity or salvation plans beyond the revelation given in Christ. Nevertheless, the line of prophetic ministry, which focused in on Jesus and is fundamentally fulfilled in him, extends out again from him, through his apostles and their agents, to duly authorized preachers in the post-apostolic age – all of whom act as delegates and agents of Jesus, the great Prophet. This progression begins as Jesus designates and sends out his apostles as preachers. We have seen a wide range of evidence demonstrating that the Gospels and Acts present Jesus and his apostles as prophetic figures. And we have seen that Paul reflects a prophetic self-understanding in his epistles at various points (not least in Rom. 10 and 2 Cor. 2 – 6).

Paul indicates in a variety of ways that this progression continues beyond the apostles. In Romans 10, the 'prophetic' preaching of the gospel by commissioned heralds is not merely his personal task, but is the normal mechanism by which the gospel will reach the nations. In 2 Corinthians 2 – 6, the 'prophetic' new-covenant ministry of the word is not Paul's alone, as though it were an exclusively apostolic privilege, but rather is shared with Timothy and Silas (2 Cor. 1:19). Were we in any doubt that this 'prophetic' preaching ministry continues beyond the apostles, Paul's commission to Timothy gives confirmation. He charges Timothy the 'man of God' (a key OT term for God's prophetic agents) to preach the apostolic and biblical word (2 Tim. 3:17; 4:2), and then to prepare others likewise to follow him in word ministry (2:2).

That Timothy's ministry stands in a line of continuity with speakers of God's word stretching back through the apostles, Jesus himself and then the Old Testament prophets should come as no surprise. Throughout the history of his dealings with his people, God has spoken to his people and led them through his word declared by his chosen agents. Given that God's word is powerful in itself, he could have provided people who would simply read his word – or he could have made provision for the Israelites to read the law for themselves privately. In his wisdom, however, he has always provided those who would be especially commissioned to proclaim his word to his people.

Those who are set apart as preachers in the church today, following on from Timothy, stand in that line of continuity that stretches from the Old Testament prophets, through Jesus, the apostles and their agents, and down through leaders of the church in the post-apostolic context. However, as we affirm that the preaching ministry assigned to Timothy and to contemporary Christian preachers stands in a line of continuity with Old Testament prophecy, we should pause to articulate what is *not meant* by such an affirmation.

First, this does not imply that preaching relies upon receiving new revelation. Old Testament prophecy relied, at least in part, on receiving new revelation from God. Often the Old Testament prophets received a direct word from God or saw a vision that they then relayed. Things have changed dramatically with the coming of Jesus, as Hebrews 1 makes clear: 'Long ago, at many times and in many ways, God spoke to our fathers by the prophets, but in these last days he has spoken to us by his Son' (Heb. 1:1–2). The final word from God in the final age of salvation history ('these last days') has been spoken in Jesus the incarnate Word of God, and we await no further new revelation concerning God's identity or salvation plans. It is true, of course, that much Old Testament prophecy was simply an exposition of the law as it applied to the situation of the people of God in the prophet's own day. Much Old Testament prophecy was fundamentally biblical exposition rather than fresh oracle, and therefore much Old Testament prophecy has a great deal in common with what preachers are to do today. Nevertheless, preaching is distinct from Old Testament prophecy in the sense that it does not bring new revelation.

Second, this affirmation does not mean that all the statements in the New Testament about new-covenant prophets or the gift of prophecy are really all about preaching. We have already noted the fact that the 'prophets' referred to in Ephesians are foundational figures who functioned alongside the apostles in the early church. The situation in 1 Corinthians 14 is more complex. Some of what is said there about prophecy sounds very much like preaching (e.g. 'the one who prophesies speaks to people for their upbuilding and encouragement and consolation', 1 Cor. 14:3). On the other hand, mention in verses 29 and 30 of 'two or three' prophets speaking and 'another' receiving 'a revelation' and being prompted to speak sounds rather unlike the central sermon at a weekly gathering.[3]

---

[3] There is neither scope nor need to enter into detailed exegesis of 1 Cor. 14 here, but the basic point to acknowledge is that the NT's various references to 'prophecy' within the church do not all necessarily refer to preaching.

Post-apostolic preachers are not given the title 'prophet' and the New Testament does not designate their preaching 'prophecy'. These observations alone indicate to us that the role of the preacher is not simply the new-covenant equivalent of the prophet in ancient Israel. The fact that the language of 'prophet' and 'prophecy' is not assigned to the Christian preacher is doubtless tied to the fact that the preacher operates under a new covenant within a different era of salvation history. In this era, Jesus the great Prophet has brought fulfilment to the prophetic message and the prophetic office.[4] Preachers today are heralds who serve Jesus the great Prophet. As they serve him, however, the New Testament sets them and their preaching ministry in a line of continuity with the prophetic office and ministry of the Old Testament which he fulfils.

Preachers must be commissioned to preach

Throughout the New Testament, preaching is normally carried out by those who have a recognized role of authority within the church and possess a commission to preach.[5] Preaching is not a generalized activity undertaken by all Christian people or on the basis of the preacher's own initiative. Jesus himself is given a divine commendation before he begins his ministry (Mark 1:11; see also 9:7). He designates and sends his apostles to preach (Mark 3:14). Paul makes it clear that Jesus will continue to commission preachers for the declaration of the gospel (Rom. 10:14–17; see also Eph. 4:11). Timothy is clearly such a one, and Paul's designation of him as a 'man of God' reflects his commission (2 Tim. 3:17; 4:2; see also 2 Tim. 1:6; 1 Tim. 4:13–14; 1 Thess. 2:4). He will, in turn, need to ensure that appropriate leaders are commissioned to carry on this ministry in Ephesus (2 Tim. 2:2; see also 1 Tim. 3:1–2). Those who are so commissioned are rightly set apart for the work of preaching and rightly receive material support (1 Cor. 9:14).

The nature of preaching uniquely reflects the nature of the gospel

This study has found that preaching in the New Testament is a public declaration of God's word by a commissioned agent that stands in a

---

[4] See Aernie's (2012: 156–157, esp. fn. 164) helpful treatment of this point with specific reference to Paul and his self-understanding, drawing upon the work of Kim and Sandnes.

[5] This does not necessarily mean that 'lay' or trainee preachers should not have opportunity to preach (indeed, this will surely be necessary in order to test a person's gifts for preaching before a formal commissioning), but it does preclude self-appointed preachers presuming to preach without appropriate invitation or commission from the church.

line of continuity with Old Testament prophetic ministry. These features of preaching set the activity apart from other forms of word ministry. Preaching is not a conversation or an exploration, but a *declaration* of a God-given message. The designation of the preached message as the 'word of hearing' or the 'hearing' (Heb. 4:2; Rom. 10:16; 1 Thess. 2:13) points to its special character as a message that is designed to be declared and then heard. This characteristic of preaching – a word that is to be proclaimed by the preacher and received by its hearers – reflects the very nature of the gospel as something graciously given by God and received by his people through hearing and believing. Unlike other less formal forms of communicating the word (through personal conversation, group discussion, etc.), the public declaration of the gospel to a group of listening people by a herald who represents God uniquely reflects God's sole agency in achieving and offering salvation.

Preaching is a divine and human activity that constitutes an encounter with God

A number of the New Testament texts we have studied have presented God as the primary agent in preaching with the implication that he is personally involved – *even personally present* – in and through the preaching of his word. In Romans 10, we saw that Paul expects people to hear Christ himself as his commissioned agents preach his word (Rom. 10:14). The 'word of Christ' proclaimed is not simply a word about Christ, but a word that Christ has spoken and continues to speak through his heralds (Rom. 10:17). In 1 Corinthians 1 – 2 Paul insists that his preaching of the 'word of the cross', which may have seemed weak in human terms, was nonetheless 'the power of God' (1 Cor. 1:18), constituting a 'demonstration of the Spirit and of power' (2:4). In fact, the human weakness of Paul's preaching ensured that the resultant faith rested 'not . . . in the wisdom of men but in the power of God' (2:5), who was the all-powerful agent behind Paul's preaching. The agency of God in the preaching of his word is evident again throughout much of Paul's discussion of the new-covenant ministry of proclamation in 2 Corinthians. Paul affirms that Jesus Christ 'was proclaimed through us' (1:19), with God clearly working by his Spirit in the lives of his people through that proclamation (1:20–22). As his heralds proclaim his word, God 'through [them] spreads the fragrance of the knowledge of him' (2:14). Paul recognizes that, as he and his associates serve as God's ambassadors, God is 'making his appeal through us' (5:20). Although Paul and his ministry associates are preachers, they also stand alongside the people of God whom they address as recipients of God's self-revelation in Christ by his Spirit, even beholding the manifest glory of God through the ministry of his word (3:16–18).[6]

In 1 Thessalonians 1, Paul recounts how their gospel came to the Thessalonians, not simply as information – as a 'word' – 'but also in power and in the Holy Spirit and with full conviction' (1:5). In other words, as Paul and his companions preached the gospel, God himself was present and at work by his Spirit (see also 1 Thess. 2:13).

The writer of Hebrews reflects similar convictions. He believes that God's voice is heard through his sermon (see the repeated refrain, 'Today, if you hear his voice . . .', 3:7, 15; 4:7) as God addresses his people from heaven (12:25). When God addresses his people through the preached word, they encounter him as Judge (4:12–13), but are at the same time encouraged to approach him through Christ the priestly mediator (4:14–16; 10:19–22).

Preaching has a natural context and particular significance within the Christian assembly

Preaching characteristically takes place in a public context in the New Testament. In the ministry of Jesus and the apostles in the Gospels and Acts, these contexts are quite varied, and a number are not specified in much detail. However, it is striking that both Jesus and the apostles frequently gravitated towards the synagogues in the towns where they were preaching (or the temple, in the case of Jerusalem), as though that were the most obvious place to preach God's word, in the first instance at least.

We have found already that new-covenant preaching stands in a line of continuity with prophetic ministry throughout the Bible. As we look back through Scripture to the archetypal prophetic addresses (or 'sermons') by the archetypal Old Testament prophet, Moses, we see a foundation for this pattern. In the wilderness at Sinai, Moses went up the mountain to receive God's covenant word and then declared it to the gathered assembly at the bottom of the mountain (see e.g. Exod. 35:1, 4, 20; Deut. 18:16). The Lord instructed Moses that this was to be the context in which his word would go out: 'Gather the people to me, that I may let them hear my words' (Deut. 4:10).

---

[6] Paul's teaching concerning the nature of new-covenant preaching ministry in 2 Cor. 3 – 4 sets something of an agenda for such ministry: namely, to behold Christ in his glory, that his people might be transformed into his image.

The Greek translation of the Old Testament (the LXX) identifies this gathering using the Greek term *ekklēsia*, which in the New Testament is translated 'church'.[7] The Lord promises through Moses that he will raise up another prophet to address his people as Moses did at the assembly in the wilderness:

> The LORD your God will raise up for you a prophet like me from among you, from your brothers – it is to him you shall listen . . . 'And I will put my words in his mouth, and he shall speak to them all that I command him.' (Deut. 18:15, 18)

Jesus is, of course, that promised Prophet.

In Judaism in Jesus' day, the people of Israel gathered at the 'synagogue' (the Greek verb *synagagein*, from which the name is derived, means 'to assemble') to hear God's word. It was entirely natural that Jesus should open his ministry by addressing the local 'assembly' of the people of Israel in his home town, and that the synagogue should so often be the first port of call for the proclamation of the gospel in any given place. This is just what we might have expected, given the promise of Deuteronomy 18.

In his discussion of the nature of new-covenant preaching ministry in 2 Corinthians 3:12–18 Paul recalls the ministry of Moses to the assembly in the wilderness and clearly refers to the ministry of the word to the gathered people at the temple and the synagogue in contemporary Judaism. New-covenant ministry is not contrasted with old-covenant ministry in this respect. The passage assumes a parallel context for the ministry: the gathered people of God. With such a context in view, Paul attests to a corporate response to the proclamation of the word: 'That is why it is through him that we utter our Amen to God for his glory' (2 Cor. 1:20).

The Hebrews sermon again belongs within the context of the regular Christian assembly. It is called a 'word of exhortation' (13:22), which was the name given to homilies in the synagogue (Acts 13:15).

Given what we have suggested concerning the nature of Christian preaching, it is not hard to see why preaching has a natural home and special significance within the Christian assembly. The church is formed and sustained through the word of God, and it is through the

---

[7] Moses repeatedly refers back to that occasion as the 'day of the assembly [*ekklēsias*]' in LXX Deuteronomy (Deut. 4:10; 9:10; 18:16). I am indebted here to Christopher Ash's exploration of the theme of 'assembly' in Scripture and its implications for the theology of preaching (Ash 2009: 75–90).

preaching of the word especially that God addresses his people and meets with them. It was as a gathered people hearing the proclamation of the word that God's people in the wilderness saw a faint reflection of God's glory in the face of Moses, and it is *particularly* as a gathered people of God hearing the proclamation of his word that God's people today behold the glory of the Lord.

This local and earthly 'assembly' of God's people mirrors the heavenly assembly (Heb. 12:22–25), which itself is presented in comparison to the assembly in the wilderness (Heb. 12:18–21). In Hebrews 12:18–25, the writer presents in a nutshell the great sweep of the biblical-theological development of the idea of 'assembly', from that first assembly in the wilderness, to its ultimate fulfilment in the heavenly city. Within the progression of God's salvation purposes, the Christian assembly addressed by the Hebrews sermon (and with it, the local Christian assembly today) stands between those two great assemblies. For God's people here on earth, so much of the experience of the heavenly assembly in Zion remains a future reality. However, there is one experience we on earth share in common with God's people gathered in heaven: as we gather in an earthly assembly to hear God's word proclaimed, we hear the same God addressing us from heaven through his word (Heb. 12:25). And so the experience of hearing the proclamation of God's word alongside God's people in the local church is nothing less than a foretaste of heaven.

Preaching is related to, but distinct from, other ministries of the word

We noted earlier that the New Testament contains no instruction or command addressed to non-leaders to 'proclaim' or 'preach' the gospel. This fact is initially surprising and requires an explanation. The lack of such a mandate could lead to the erroneous conclusion that the New Testament envisages no role for non-leaders in word ministry. If we understood the language of preaching in the New Testament to refer to word ministry in general (rather than to the authoritative public proclamation of the word by a commissioned leader), we might be forced to adopt such a position. However, if we accept (as this study has found) that the verbs *euangelizomai, katangellō* and *kēryssō* are specialist terms in the New Testament that normally refer to preaching as a particular type of word ministry, we are led to conclude that not all Christian believers are given a mandate to preach, while still allowing for the possibility that the New Testament may well mandate other forms of word ministry for non-leaders.

And that, of course, is just what we have found to be the case. Preaching is not the sole ministry of the word mandated by the New Testament, but rather forms part – albeit a distinct and highly significant part – of the variety of word ministries envisaged for the post-apostolic era. The findings of this study concerning the distinctive nature and significance of preaching suggest that the preaching of the word of God should drive and fuel the other word ministries within the church. This conclusion is bolstered by our brief observations concerning the word ministries of all believers in the epistles. Analysis of some of the clearest examples we found in the epistles (in Colossians, 1 Thessalonians, Titus and Hebrews) of non-leaders being charged to engage in forms of word ministry revealed that their varied ministries were expected to function in parallel with, and derive from, the preaching ministry of the leaders.

Final reflections

As the Introduction acknowledged, this volume does not pretend to be a comprehensive study of what the Bible, the New Testament or even the epistles have to say about preaching. From what we have found, however, it seems possible – even necessary – to affirm this much: the public proclamation of the word of God in the Christian assembly has a clear mandate from Scripture and occupies a place of central importance in the life of the local church. Preaching is necessary and vital – but not all-sufficient – for the nourishment and edification of the local church. All God's people are ministers of his word, and a healthy church will be a church where all kinds of word ministries (formal and informal) flourish and abound. However, none of those other ministries of the word can take the place of the public preaching of God's word. The primary feeding and teaching of God's people should come from the preaching that takes place week by week in the assembly. That preaching ministry should, in turn, fuel and shape many other ministries of the word, as all believers speak (and sing!) the word to each other and to those outside the church.

The preaching of the word of God is God's gracious gift to his people. It is a gift by which he speaks to us, encounters us, equips us for ministry, and, through the power of his Spirit, transforms us – all for his glory.

Bibliography

Adam, P. (1996), *Speaking God's Words: A Practical Theology of Preaching*, Leicester: Inter-Varsity Press.

Aernie, J. W. (2012), *Is Paul Also Among the Prophets? An Examination of the Relationship between Paul and the Old Testament Prophetic Tradition in 2 Corinthians*, LNTS 467, London: T&T Clark.

Ash, C. (2009), *The Priority of Preaching*, Fearn: Christian Focus.

——— (2011), *Hearing the Spirit: Knowing the Father through the Son*, Fearn: Christian Focus.

Austin, J. L. (1975), *How to Do Things with Words*, 2nd edn, Oxford: Oxford University Press.

Barnett, P. (1997), *The Second Epistle to the Corinthians*, NICNT, Grand Rapids/Cambridge: Eerdmans.

Barr, J. (1961), *The Semantics of Biblical Language*, Oxford: Oxford University Press.

Barrett, C. K. (1991), *The Epistle to the Romans*, BNTC, 2nd edn, London: A&C Black.

Beckwith, R. (2003), *Elders in Every City: The Origin and Role of the Ordained Ministry*, Carlisle: Paternoster.

Bock, D. L. (1994), *Luke*, IVPNTC, Downers Grove: InterVarsity Press; Leicester: Inter-Varsity Press.

Bowers, P. (1987), 'Fulfilling the Gospel: the Scope of the Pauline Mission', *JETS* 30.2: 195–198.

——— (1991), 'Church and Mission in Paul', *JSNT* 44: 89–111.

Bruce, F. F. (1982a), *The Epistle to the Galatians: A Commentary on the Greek Text*, NIGTC, Carlisle: Paternoster.

——— (1982b), *1 & 2 Thessalonians*, WBC 45, Nashville: Thomas Nelson.

Bullinger, E. W. (1908), *A Critical Lexicon and Concordance to the English and Greek New Testament*, 5th rev. edn, London: Longmans, Green & Co.

Carson, D. A. (1995), *Matthew Chapters 1 through 12*, EBC, Grand Rapids: Zondervan.

——— (2014), 'Do the Work of an Evangelist', *Them* 39.1: 1–4.

Ciampa, R. E. (1998), *The Presence and Function of Scripture in Galatians 1 and 2*, WUNT 2.102, Tübingen: Mohr Siebeck.

Ciampa, R. E., and B. S. Rosner (2010), *The First Letter to the Corinthians*, PNTC, Grand Rapids: Eerdmans; Nottingham: Apollos.

Cockerill, G. L. (2012), *The Epistle to the Hebrews*, NICNT, Grand Rapids/Cambridge: Eerdmans.

Cotterell, P., and M. Turner (1989), *Linguistics and Biblical Interpretation*, London: SPCK.

Cranfield, C. E. B. (1985a), 'Changes in Person and Number', in C. E. B. Cranfield, *The Bible and Christian Life: A Collection of Essays*, Edinburgh: T&T Clark, 215–228.

—— (1985b), *Romans: A Shorter Commentary*, Grand Rapids/ Cambridge: Eerdmans.

Croatto, J. S. (2005), 'Jesus, Prophet Like Elijah, and Prophet-Teacher Like Moses in Luke–Acts', *JBL* 124.3: 451–465.

Dever, M., and G. Gilbert (2012), *Preach: Theology Meets Practice*, IX Marks, Nashville: B&H Publishing Group.

Dickson, J. P. (2003), *Mission-Commitment in Ancient Judaism and in the Pauline Communities: The Shape, Extent and Background of Early Christian Mission*, WUNT 2.159, Tübingen: Mohr Siebeck.

—— (2005), 'Gospel As News: εὐαγγελ- from Aristophanes to the Apostle Paul', *NTS* 51.2: 212–230.

Dodd, C. H. (1936), *The Apostolic Preaching and Its Developments*, London: Hodder & Stoughton.

Dunn, J. D. G. (1988), *Romans 9 – 16*, WBC 38B, Dallas: Word.

Edsall, B. A. (2014), *Paul's Witness to Formative Early Christian Instruction*, WUNT 2.365, Tübingen: Mohr Siebeck.

Ellis, E. E. (1971), 'Paul and His Co-Workers', *NTS* 17.4: 437–452.

Evans, C. A. (1981), '"Preacher" and "Preaching": Some Lexical Observations', *JETS* 24.4: 315–322.

Fee, G. D. (1987), *The First Epistle to the Corinthians*, NICNT, Grand Rapids/Cambridge: Eerdmans.

—— (2009), *The First and Second Letters to the Thessalonians*, NICNT, Grand Rapids/Cambridge: Eerdmans.

France, R. T. (2007), *The Gospel of Matthew*, NIGTC, Grand Rapids/ Cambridge: Eerdmans.

Gaventa, B. R. (2011), 'The Mission of God in Paul's Letter to the Romans', in Trevor Burke and Brian S. Rosner (eds.), *Paul As Missionary: Identity, Activity, Theology, and Practice*, London: T&T Clark, 65–75.

Gignilliat, M. (2007), *Paul and Isaiah's Servants: Paul's Theological Reading of Isaiah 40 – 66 in 2 Corinthians 5.14 – 6.10*, LNTS 330, London: T&T Clark.

Gilliard, F. D. (1994), 'Paul and the Killing of the Prophets in 1 Thess. 2:15', *NovT* 36.3: 259–270.

Green, G. L. (2002), *The Letters to the Thessalonians*, PNTC, Grand Rapids: Eerdmans; Leicester: Apollos.

Griffiths, J. I. (2014), *Hebrews and Divine Speech*, LNTS 507, London: Bloomsbury T&T Clark.

Grumm, M. H. (1970), 'Translating Kēryssō and Related Verbs', *BT* 21.4: 176–179.

Hafemann, S. J. (2000a), *Suffering and Ministry in the Spirit: Paul's Defence of His Ministry in II Corinthians 2:14 – 3:3*, PBTM, Carlisle: Paternoster.

—————— (2000b), *2 Corinthians*, NIVAC, Grand Rapids: Zondervan.

—————— (2005), *Paul, Moses, and the History of Israel: The Letter/Spirit Contrast and the Argument from Scripture in 2 Corinthians 3*, PBM, Milton Keynes: Paternoster.

Harris, M. J. (2005), *The Second Epistle to the Corinthians*, NIGTC, Grand Rapids: Eerdmans; Milton Keynes: Paternoster.

Hawthorne, G. F., and R. P. Martin (2004), *Philippians*, rev. edn, WBC 43, Nashville: Thomas Nelson.

Holstein, J. A. (1977), 'The Case of "*'īš hā'ĕlōhīm*" Reconsidered: Philological Analysis versus Historical Reconstruction', *HUCA* 48: 69–81.

Jewett, R. (1970), 'Conflicting Movements in the Early Church as Reflected in Philippians', *NovT* 12.4: 362–390.

Johnson, L. T. (2006), *Hebrews: A Commentary*, NTL, Louisville: Westminster John Knox Press.

Keller, T. (2015), *Preaching: Communicating Faith in an Age of Skepticism*, London: Hodder & Stoughton.

Kelly, J. N. D. (1963), *A Commentary on the Pastoral Epistles: I Timothy, II Timothy, Titus*, BNTC, London: A&C Black.

Keown, M. J. (2008), *Congregational Evangelism in Philippians: The Centrality of an Appeal for Gospel Proclamation to the Fabric of Philippians*, PBM, Milton Keynes: Paternoster.

Klein, W. W., C. L. Blomberg and R. L. Hubbard, Jr. (2004), *Introduction to Biblical Interpretation*, rev. edn, Nashville: Thomas Nelson.

Knight, G. W. III (1992), *The Pastoral Epistles*, NIGTC, Grand Rapids/Cambridge: Eerdmans.

Köstenberger, A. J., and P. T. O'Brien (2001), *Salvation to the Ends of the Earth: A Biblical Theology of Mission*, NSBT, Leicester: Apollos; Downers Grove: InterVarsity Press.

Kruse, C. G. (2012), *Paul's Letter to the Romans*, PNTC, Grand Rapids: Eerdmans; Nottingham: Apollos.

Lim, T. H. (1987), 'Not in Persuasive Words of Wisdom, But in the Demonstration of the Spirit and Power', *NovT* 29.2: 137–149.

Litfin, D. (2015), *Paul's Theology of Preaching: The Apostle's Challenge to the Art of Persuasion in Ancient Corinth*, Downers Grove: IVP Academic.

Liubinskas, S. (2013), 'The Body of Christ in Mission: Paul's Ecclesiology and the Role of the Church in Mission', *Miss.* 41.4: 402–415.

McDonald, J. I. H. (1980), *Kerygma and Didache: The Articulation and Structure of the Earliest Christian Message*, SNTSMS 37, Cambridge: Cambridge University Press.

Marshall, I. H. (2000), 'Who Were the Evangelists?', in Jostein Ådna and Hans Kvalbein (eds.), *The Mission of the Early Church to Jews and Gentiles*, WUNT 127, Tübingen: Mohr Siebeck, 251–263.

Martin, R. P. (1986), *2 Corinthians*, WBC 40, Waco: Word.

Meyer, J. C. (2013), *Preaching: A Biblical Theology*, Wheaton: Crossway.

Mitchell, M. M. (1994), 'Rhetorical Shorthand in Pauline Argumentation: The Functions of "the Gospel" in the Corinthian Correspondence', in L. Ann Jervis and Peter Richardson (eds.), *Gospel in Paul: Studies on Corinthians, Galatians and Romans for Richard N. Longenecker*, JSNTSS 108, Sheffield: Sheffield Academic Press, 63–68.

Moo, D. J. (1996), *The Epistle to the Romans*, NICNT, Grand Rapids/Cambridge: Eerdmans.

Morris, L. (1988), *The Epistle to the Romans*, Grand Rapids: Eerdmans; Leicester: Inter-Varsity Press.

——— (1991), *The First and Second Epistles to the Thessalonians*, NICNT, rev. edn, Grand Rapids/Cambridge: Eerdmans.

Moule, C. F. D. (1963), *An Idiom-Book of New Testament Greek*, Cambridge: Cambridge University Press.

Mounce, R. H. (1960), *The Essential Nature of New Testament Preaching*, Grand Rapids: Eerdmans.

Mounce, W. D. (2000), *Pastoral Epistles*, WBC 46, Nashville: Thomas Nelson.

O'Brien, P. T. (1991), *The Epistle to the Philippians: A Commentary on the Greek Text*, NIGTC, Grand Rapids: Eerdmans.

—— (1993), *Consumed by Passion: Paul and the Dynamic of the Gospel*, Homebush West, NSW: Lancer. [Re-published in 1995 as *Gospel and Mission in the Writings of Paul: An Exegetical and Theological Analysis*, Grand Rapids: Baker; Carlisle: Paternoster.]

—— (1999), *The Letter to the Ephesians*, PNTC, Grand Rapids: Eerdmans; Leicester: Apollos.

—— (2010), *The Letter to the Hebrews*, PNTC, Grand Rapids: Eerdmans; Nottingham: Apollos.

Old, H. O. (1998), *The Reading and Preaching of the Scriptures in the Worship of the Christian Church*, Vol. 1: *The Biblical Period*, Grand Rapids/Cambridge: Eerdmans.

Peterson, D. G. (2009), *The Acts of the Apostles*, PNTC, Grand Rapids: Eerdmans; Nottingham: Apollos.

—— (2011), 'Prophetic Preaching in the Book of Acts', in Paul A. Barker, Richard J. Condie and Andrew S. Malone (eds.), *Serving God's Words: Windows on Preaching and Ministry*, Nottingham: Inter-Varsity Press, 32–52.

Plummer, R. L. (2006), *Paul's Understanding of the Church's Mission: Did the Apostle Paul Expect the Early Christian Communities to Evangelize?*, PBM, Milton Keynes: Paternoster.

Runia, K. (1978), 'What Is Preaching According to the New Testament?', *TynBul* 29: 3–48.

Samra, J. G. (2006), *Being Conformed to Christ in Community: A Study of Maturity, Maturation and the Local Church in the Undisputed Pauline Epistles*, London: T&T Clark.

Sanday, W., and A. Headlam (1920), *A Critical and Exegetical Commentary on the Epistle to the Romans*, ICC, 5th edn, Edinburgh: T&T Clark.

Sandnes, K. O. (1991), *Paul: One of the Prophets?*, WUNT 2.43, Tübingen: Mohr Siebeck.

Schreiner, T. R. (2010), *Galatians*, ZECNT, Grand Rapids: Zondervan.

Smillie, G. R. (2005), '"The Other ΛΟΓΟΣ" at the End of Heb. 4:13', *NovT* 47.1: 19–25.

Smith, C. S. (2012), *Pauline Communities as 'Scholastic Communities'*, WUNT 2.335, Tübingen: Mohr Siebeck.

Stott, J. (1961), *The Preacher's Portrait*, London: Tyndale.

—— (1994), *The Message of Romans*, BST, Leicester: Inter-Varsity Press.

Stowers, S. K. (1984), 'Social Status, Public Speaking and Private Teaching: The Circumstances of Paul's Preaching Activity', *NovT* 26.1: 59–82.

Thayer, J. H. (1896), *Thayer's Greek–English Lexicon of the New Testament*, 4th edn, Edinburgh: T&T Clark.

Thrall, M. (1994, 2000), *A Critical and Exegetical Commentary on the Second Epistle to the Corinthians*, 2 vols, ICC, London: T&T Clark International.

Vanhoye, A. (1989), *Structure and Message of the Epistle to the Hebrews*, tr. J. Swetnam, SubBi 12, Rome: Pontificio Instituto Biblico.

Wallace, D. B. (1996), *Greek Grammar Beyond the Basics: An Exegetical Syntax of the New Testament*, Grand Rapids: Zondervan.

Ward, T. (2009), *Words of Life: Scripture As the Living and Active Word of God*, Nottingham: Inter-Varsity Press.

Ware, J. P. (1992), 'The Thessalonians As a Missionary Congregation: 1 Thessalonians 1,5–8', *ZNW* 83: 126–131.

————— (2005), *The Mission of the Church in Paul's Letter to the Philippians in the Context of Ancient Judaism*, NovTSup 120, Leiden: Brill.

Winter, B. W. (1993), 'The Entries and Ethics of Orators and Paul (1 Thessalonians 2:1–12)', *TynBul* 44: 55–74.

————— (2002), *Philo and Paul among the Sophists: Alexandrian and Corinthian Responses to a Julio-Claudian Movement*, 2nd edn, Grand Rapids/Cambridge: Eerdmans.

Wright, N. T. (1996), *Jesus and the Victory of God*, vol. 2, London: SPCK.

Index of authors

Index of Scripture references

144

Acts (*cont.*)
20:25 *30, 39*
22:5 *18n8*
22:12 *18n8*
22:26 *18n6*
23:11 *18n8*
23:16 *18n6*
23:17 *18n6*
23:19 *18n6*
26:5 *18n8*
26:20 *18, 18n6*
26:22 *18n8*
26:23 *26*
28:21 *18n6*
28:31 *30, 32, 39*

Romans
1:4–5 *72*
1:8 *26–27*
1:15 *22, 34, 35n34*
1:16 *34–5n34*
2:21 *30*
3:21 *18n8*
10 *67–73, 122, 123, 126, 127*
10:2 *18n8*
10:3 *67*
10:5 *67*
10:6–8 *68*
10:8 *30, 70*
10:9–13 *68*
10:14 *30, 71, 126, 130*
10:14–15 *65n16, 70, 72*
10:14–17 *129*
10:14–18 *70n6*
10:15 *22, 30, 71n15*
10:16 *65n16, 68, 70, 113, 130*
10:16–17 *71*
10:17 *69, 71, 99, 130*
10:18 *69*
11:1 *67*
11:5–18 *67n*
15:20 *22, 65n16*

15:21 *65n16*
16:25 *32*

1 Corinthians
1 – 2 *130*
1:10–12 *76*
1:13–16 *76*
1:17 *22, 36, 75, 75n2, 76, 80, 122*
1:17–25 *77*
1:17b *78*
1:18 *76, 130*
1:18–31 *76–7*
1:20 *77*
1:21 *32, 75*
1:22 *77*
1:23 *30, 35n38, 75, 75n2, 77*
2:1 *26, 75, 75n2*
2:1–4 *36n40*
2:2 *80, 122*
2:4 *32, 35n38, 75, 130*
2:5 *78, 130*
2:10–13 *75n2*
3:1–3 *75n2*
3:9 *75n2*
4:9–10 *75n2*
4:15 *75*
4:17 *84n1*
9 *78–79, 80*
9:1–14 *79*
9:7 *79*
9:8–12 *79*
9:12 *75, 80*
9:13 *79*
9:14 *26, 34–5, 75, 79, 129*
9:14–27 *36n40*
9:15–18 *80n*
9:16 *22, 75, 80*
9:17 *80*
9:18 *22, 75*
9:22 *80*
9:23 *75*
9:27 *30, 35n38, 75*

10 – 13 *76n5*
11:26 *26, 27, 75*
14 *33n32*
14:3 *128*
14:16 *85n6*
14:24 *18n6*
14:29–30 *128*
15:1 *22, 75*
15:1–2 *80*
15:1–14 *36n40*
15:2 *22, 75, 81*
15:3–5 *80, 122*
15:11 *31, 35n38, 75*
15:12 *31, 35n38, 75, 81*
15:14 *32, 35n38, 75*
15:15 *18n8, 81*
16:19–20 *42n5*

2 Corinthians
1:1 *84*
1:12–14 *83*
1:15–24 *84n2*
1:19 *31, 84, 85, 88, 126, 127, 130*
1:20 *85, 88n14, 132*
1:20–22 *130*
1:21–22 *88*
2 – 6 *127*
2:12 *85*
2:12 – 6:13 *83–95*
2:14 *88–89, 130*
2:14–17 *86*
2:16 *93, 94*
2:17 *83, 88–89*
3 *122*
3 – 4 *131n*
3:1–2 *89*
3:1–6 *83*
3:3 *89*
3:4–6 *93*
3:5–6 *89*
3:6 *84*
3:7 *87, 90*
3:7–11 *86*

146

Titles in this series:

An index of Scripture references for all the volumes may be found at
http://www.thegospelcoalition.org/resources/nsbt

Finding the Textbook You Need

The IVP Academic Textbook Selector
is an online tool for instantly finding the IVP books
suitable for over 250 courses across 24 disciplines.

---

ivpacademic.com